"Insightful, transformational read as a business leader, husband and father!"

Colin Hunter, Group Managing Director,
Potential Squared International

"This powerful book has been further simplified and illuminated by Jamie Smart's fresh understanding of the beauty of the human mind."

Steve Chandler, Author of *Time Warrior*

"The principles that Jamie Smart describes so elegantly and well, are very simple. Don't underestimate their power. Take your time with this little book. The wisdom in it changes everything."

Sandra Krot, Director of Learning, Insight Principles

"*The Little Book of Clarity* does an excellent job of explaining the basic psychological principles at the core of everyone's work and personal life. Realizing these principles can be truly transformative for you, your team and your company. This book can be a real help in that process."

Ken Manning, PhD, President of Insight Principles

"*The Little Book of Clarity* will take you to the essence of who you really are, and give you the certainty to be whatever you wish."

Cathy Casey, M.A., Principle Based Consultant

"I love what Jamie Smart has presented in *The Little Book of Clarity*. If you are searching for the wisdom, happiness, and well being that lies within you then this book will be a wonderful guide."

Mark Howard, PhD, Three Principles Institute

"*The Little Book of Clarity* is an insider's guide to the psychological paradigm-shift that has profound implications for your performance, your relationships and your life as a whole."

Chantal Burns, Performance Coach, Bestselling Author of
*Instant Motivation: The surprising truth behind what really
drives top performance*

THE
LITTLE BOOK
OF
CLARITY

A quick guide to focus and declutter your mind

Jamie Smart

CAPSTONE
A Wiley Brand

This edition first published 2015

© 2015 Jamie Smart
CLARITY® is a registered trademark of Jamie Smart Limited

This is an abridged and revised edition of *Clarity*, published 2013, ISBN: 9780857084484

Registered office
John Wiley and Sons Ltd, The Atrium, Southern Gate, Chichester, West Sussex, PO19 8SQ, United Kingdom

For details of our global editorial offices, for customer services and for information about how to apply for permission to reuse the copyright material in this book please see our website at www.wiley.com.

The right of the author to be identified as the author of this work has been asserted in accordance with the Copyright, Designs and Patents Act 1988.

Reprinted March 2015

Wiley publishes in a variety of print and electronic formats and by print-on-demand. Some material included with standard print versions of this book may not be included in e-books or in print-on-demand. If this book refers to media such as a CD or DVD that is not included in the version you purchased, you may download this material at http://booksupport.wiley.com. For more information about Wiley products, visit www.wiley.com.

Designations used by companies to distinguish their products are often claimed as trademarks. All brand names and product names used in this book and on its cover are trade names, service marks, trademark or registered trademarks of their respective owners. The publisher and the book are not associated with any product or vendor mentioned in this book. None of the companies referenced within the book have endorsed the book.

Limit of Liability/Disclaimer of Warranty: While the publisher and author have used their best efforts in preparing this book, they make no representations or warranties with the respect to the accuracy or completeness of the contents of this book and specifically disclaim any implied warranties of merchantability or fitness for a particular purpose. It is sold on the understanding that the publisher is not engaged in rendering professional services and neither the publisher nor the author shall be liable for damages arising herefrom. If professional advice or other expert assistance is required, the services of a competent professional should be sought.

Library of Congress Cataloging-in-Publication Data

Smart, Jamie
    The little book of clarity : a quick guide to focus and declutter your mind / Jamie Smart.
        pages cm
    Includes bibliographical references and index.
    ISBN 978-0-857-08606-8 (pbk. : alk. paper)   1. Insight.   2. Attention.   3. Thought and thinking.   4. Decision making.   I. Title.
    BF449.5.S63 2015
    153.4–dc23

                                                                                    2014047602

A catalogue record for this book is available from the British Library.

ISBN 978-0-857-08606-8 (paperback) ISBN 978-0-857-08604-4 (ebk)

ISBN 978-0-857-08605-1 (ebk)

Cover design: Wiley

Set in 10/13pt SabonLTStd-Roman by Aptara, New Delhi, India

Printed in Great Britain by TJ International Ltd, Padstow, Cornwall, UK

To the pioneering community of Clarity coaches, practitioners, trainers and consultants...

Contents

. . . .

Preface

··

This book's predecessor, *CLARITY: Clear Mind, Better Performance, Bigger Results*, evoked a "Marmite" response when it was launched in early 2013. Many people loved CLARITY (the book became an international number 1 bestseller, a gratifying response for any author). But while the majority of Amazon reviewers gave the book 5 stars, explaining how CLARITY had transformed their lives, a full 10% of reviewers gave the book 1 star, with criticisms ranging from "too simplistic" to "too complicated" and various points in between.

This polarity was not unexpected. I've been sharing the principles behind clarity with individuals and groups since 2009, and the response to the book mirrors those of my public speaking audiences. In fact, it's quite predictable given the core message of *CLARITY* – that a clear mind is your natural state, and there's nothing you need to *do* to clear it; that our misguided attempts to clear the mind often result in more of what was clouding them in the *first* place. This assertion flies in the face of the personal development norm of telling people "what and how to think and do" in order to have the results you desire.

But some of the most fascinating feedback began arriving six months *after* the book's publication. People started coming up to me after talks and telling me in hushed tones that when they first read *CLARITY*, it hadn't made sense to them, but when they went back to the book a few months later, something strange had happened. They discovered that it not only made sense, but that they'd incorporated the lessons from their *first* time reading the book *without even realizing it.*

This makes perfect sense. While most personal development approaches offer "additive" advice (tips, techniques and concepts to remember, practice and apply) the principles behind clarity are ruthlessly subtractive...

Understanding these principles takes things *off* your mind rather than giving you more to think about.

The revelation that the mind is a self-correcting system resonated deeply with many people. Liverpool striker, Daniel Sturridge, scored his first Premier League hat-trick against Fulham in May 2013, then arrived at his post-match interview carrying a copy of *CLARITY*. One of my clients, Bluecrest Health Screening, started including a *CLARITY Quotient* section in their screenings, empowering corporate clients to take charge of their engagement and stress levels. Demand for training in the principles behind clarity has continued to increase, and a growing community of professionals are being certified as clarity coaches, practitioners and trainers.

Which brings us to an important question: *Why a little book of CLARITY?*

The acceleration of technology, information and communication has continued to increase since *CLARITY* was published. People are even busier and assailed by even greater demands on their precious time and attention. In the face of this, the idea of a concise version of *CLARITY* pared down to the bare essentials started becoming more and more attractive. It would provide an opportunity for me to further simplify and clarify the central message of the book, and to refine some of the terminology. Perhaps most importantly, it would mean that new readers could be introduced to the principles behind *CLARITY*, and start experiencing the benefits in their work, their relationships and their lives as a whole.

Believe it or not, I receive messages most days from people telling me what an enormous difference understanding these principles has made in their lives. While some have found new relationships, careers and life circumstances, the more universal discoveries are new peace of mind, clarity and freedom. The promises of a clear mind, better performance and bigger results are underpinned by something that's there for all of us: the discovery of where your experience is coming from, what you're up to in life and who you really are.

To your increasing clarity!
Jamie Smart, 2015

Introduction

....

"What information consumes is rather obvious: it consumes the attention of its recipients."

Herbert Simon, Economist, winner of the Nobel Prize
in Economics, 1978

"If a pond is clouded with mud, there's nothing you can do to make the water clear. But when you allow the mud to settle, it will clear on its own, because clarity is the water's natural state..."

Clarity is your *mind's* natural state.

For many years, I've been sharing this simple metaphor in workshops and seminars with business leaders, entrepreneurs, coaches, consultants, therapists and private individuals. As people allow their mud to settle, clarity emerges, and they discover they have what they need for the job at hand.

So what is clarity, and why does it matter? How does clarity work, and why do so many people struggle to find it? Most importantly,

THE LITTLE BOOK OF CLARITY

how can you find the clarity you need and start benefiting from it?

It's well known that outstanding leaders in every field, from Olympic medal-winners to visionary entrepreneurs, profit from the flow-states that a clear mind brings. With clarity of mind comes the qualities that drive sustainable results. These qualities and results are what individuals and organizations are searching for. But, due to a simple misunderstanding, we've been looking in the wrong place until now.

The purpose of this book is to correct the misunderstanding and help you experience greater and greater clarity, with all the benefits it provides. The book asks and answers the following questions:

1 *What is clarity?* It turns out that clarity is a kind of "universal resource". When we have a clear head, we have everything we need for the job at hand. Ask a nervous speaker what's going through their mind when they're onstage, and they'll explain their fears, worries and anxieties. Ask a *confident* speaker what they're thinking about onstage and the answer's almost always consistent: "Nothing!" This is the case in every field of high performance, from the classroom to the playing field, from the boardroom to the bedroom; when you've got nothing on your mind, you're free to give your best.

2 *Why is clarity essential?* You're going to discover why clarity is so important for living a life that's successful on the *inside* as well as on the outside. It turns out that many of

the most desirable qualities people struggle to "develop" (such as intuition, resilience, creativity, motivation, confidence and even *leadership*) are actually expressions of an *innate* capacity; they're emergent properties of an uncluttered mind. These qualities drive the results people desire. Clarity is the source of authentic leadership and high performance. It allows us to be present in the moment, and have an enjoyable experience of life. A sense of purpose, direction and entrepreneurial spirit are natural for people with a clear head. So are happiness, freedom, security, love, confidence and peace of mind.

3   *How does clarity work, and how can you get it to work for you?* You're going to be introduced to the principles behind the natural capacity for experience – thinking, feeling and perceiving – that every person is born with. This innate capacity generates 100% of our experience of life, moment to moment.

Clarity is a naturally emergent property of this capacity – it isn't something you *do*; it's something you already *have*. The mind has its own "self-clearing" function, capable of guiding you back to clarity, regardless of what state (or circumstances) you're in. While this is extremely evident in small children, all but a fortunate few have it conditioned out of them by the time they reach adulthood.

As you start to deepen your understanding of the principles behind clarity, you're going to reconnect with your mind's natural self-clearing function. As a result, you'll find that you start having a) an effortlessly clear mind, b) more time for what's important, c) improved decision making, d) better performance where it counts and e) more of the results that matter to you. Some of the "side effects" you may notice include

3

improving relationships, reducing stress levels, more passion and an increasing engagement with life.

4 *Why do we need clarity now, more than ever?* We're living at a pivotal point in history; millions of people are faced with uncertainty, complexity and increasing chaos. As individuals, as organizations and as an entire species, clarity is the key to solving the big issues that face us, if we want to create a sustainable future for ourselves, and the generations that follow us.

You see, without even realizing it, we've been using an industrial-age *misunderstanding* of how the mind works to try to deal with the challenges of a digital world. This misunderstanding gives rise to the contaminated thinking (e.g., worry, anxiety, overthinking, etc.) that obscures our innate capacity for peace, presence, high performance, creativity, security, love and the like. As you start to "see through" the misunderstanding, clarity will emerge more and more frequently and reliably. To put it succinctly: *Clarity equals capacity minus contamination.*

CLARITY   equals   **Capacity**   minus   **Contamination**

As you continue reading this book, you're going to start undoing the conditioning that's been keeping you from clarity until now, and notice yourself experiencing a clear mind more and more frequently (with all the benefits it brings). At the times when your mind *is* clouded, you'll know what to do (and more importantly, what *not* to do). The conditioning is based in three main areas:

1   *Contaminated thinking arising from the outside-in misunderstanding.* A widespread piece of conditioning mistakenly attributes clarity (and the lack of it) to a variety of circumstances. While this can easily be shown not to be the case, the misunderstanding is extremely persistent when it goes unchallenged. You're going to be introduced to a relaxing and enjoyable way of reading that will help you to "see through" this misunderstanding, and begin having insights and realizations that will make a difference to you immediately. As you deepen your understanding of the principles behind clarity, you'll find stale habits of contaminated thinking dropping away, and clarity emerging to take their place.

2   *The move from a manufacturing economy to a knowledge economy.* Just as factory workers need to keep their machines clean and well oiled, knowledge workers, coaches, creatives, managers and leaders need to take similar care of their minds. Individuals and businesses are paying the price as time-scarcity, attention-poverty and information-saturation clog the "mental machinery" we rely on. But there's good news. People are born with a powerful immune system that protects us from disease and illness. The immune system reflects an innate tendency towards health and wellness that also shows up in the body's ability to repair wounds, breaks and other injuries. It is a little-known fact, however, that people also have a "psychological immune system," able to quickly restore even an extremely perturbed mind to clarity and well-being.

As your understanding of the principles behind clarity continues to deepen, you'll find that you have what you need to prosper in times of uncertainty, complexity and change.

3   *Attempting to find clarity using outside-in methods.* The mind is a self-correcting system. The primary condition needed for a self-correcting system to find its way back to balance is simple: an absence of external interference. Outside-in methods such as positive thinking, affirmations and other techniques are examples of external interference. Other examples include smoking, drinking too much and Internet addiction. While they can be used to clear the mind in the short term, they are not sustainable. In the long run, they often make matters worse if they give the busy-minded person even more to think about and do (I'm assuming that the *last* thing you need is more on your mind).

This book is designed to *effortlessly* activate your innate capacity for clarity. As you'll find out, the principles you're going to be discovering will take care of the implementation for you.

DISTINCTION: Acting it vs. Catching it

- Acting it: *Acting* like you have a cold is neither easy nor convincing. Most business and personal development books aim at giving you the things to think, change and do so you can "act" in a certain way to get the results you want.

- Catching it: When you *catch* a cold, the symptoms emerge effortlessly because they're *real*. This book is designed so that you can "catch" an understanding that results in the "symptoms" of increasing clarity, resilience and peace of mind.

I want to assure you that you have the capacity for sustainable clarity, and all the benefits it brings. But first, a question:

Q: If you're caught in a trap, what's the one thing you have to do before you can escape?

A: You have to realize that you've been caught in a trap.

Until you realize you've been caught in a trap, you're very unlikely to get out of it. But once you know about the trap, and you can see how it works, then escape is pretty straightforward. Especially if other people have escaped from the same trap, and can show you how.

So please allow me to reveal the trap that's ensnared millions of people, including me...

keep exploring ⁜ connect with others
share your discoveries ⁜ deepen your understanding

At the end of each chapter, you'll find a section containing a "thought experiment". This is a statement or question for reflection to help you integrate what you are learning even more deeply. For example:

Thought experiment: *We each experience greater clarity from time to time. As you look back now, what are some of the more* *memorable occasions when you've found yourself experiencing an unexpected increase in clarity?*

When you reach a thought experiment, pause for a moment. You don't have to figure out the question or "get it right". You don't even have to answer it. Just reading the question and reflecting on it for a moment is enough to continue your process of integration.

This section will also contain a website URL to enter into your browser and a QR code that you can scan using your smartphone. These will take you to web pages containing material relating to the chapter you've just read, ranging from videos and audio recordings to shareable articles, photos and infographics. In addition to the resources, you'll find features that allow you to post your comments and share what you're learning with others.

Experience shows that sharing your discoveries is a simple but powerful way for you to continue integrating what you're learning, as your understanding of the principles behind clarity continues to deepen. I encourage you to explore, comment on and share these resources as you make your way through the book. You can start now…

www.LittleBookOfClarity.com/introduction

PART ONE
The Essential Foundations

1

Misunderstanding: The Hidden Trap

....

"None are more hopelessly enslaved than those who falsely believe they are free."

Johann Wolfgang von Goethe,
Poet, playwright, novelist and philosopher

"An addict is someone who's trying to use a visible solution to solve an invisible problem..."

I started drinking when I was 12 years old and didn't stop for good until I was 30. On the journey of recovery, my life improved in ways that I didn't even imagine were possible. But, in the process, I discovered an even deeper addiction at the very heart of modern culture. This addiction is so subtle, it's almost *invisible*; a life-eroding trap that has hooked countless millions of people...

The hidden hamster wheel

The hidden hamster wheel is one of the most common barriers to clarity. It's based in a misunderstanding that's taken to be "obviously true" by most people. It's so subtle and pervasive that it shows up in everything from children's books to leadership programmes; from movies to marketing campaigns.

The Power of Misunderstanding

In the 1800s, it was widely accepted that illnesses such as cholera and the plague were caused by "bad air" (also known as atmospheres or miasmas). At the time, huge numbers of people were moving to Soho in London, with an associated increase in sewage. The council of the day decided to dump the excess waste into the river Thames, unknowingly contaminating the water supply, and causing a cholera outbreak that claimed the lives of 618 Soho residents in just a few weeks.

The miasma theory was a misunderstanding that was seen as fact. As a result, the decision to pump sewage into the water supply was taken from *within* that misunderstanding. While you and I know it's crazy to let human waste anywhere near your drinking water, that's because we have a better understanding of how the world works.

Misunderstanding can lead to needless misery, suffering and even death. But as soon as people get a clearer understanding of the nature of reality *as it already is*, there can be a massive and widespread improvement in quality of life.

The life-damaging misunderstanding that I call the hidden hamster wheel is the mistaken belief that our "core states" such as security, confidence, peace, love, happiness and success can be provided or threatened by our circumstances; by something "visible".

We have this belief because we've been conditioned to believe that there's somewhere to get to, and that "there" is better than "here". And "there" comes in a variety of tantalizing flavours that look something like this:

I'll be [*happy/secure/fulfilled/peaceful/better/successful/ok*] when I...

- Find the right work/hobby/partner/community – the "there" of *doing and relationships.*

- Get the money/write the book/start the business/lose the weight – the "there" of *accomplishment.*

- Change my thinking/my limiting beliefs/do my affirmations – the "there" of *mindset.*

- Meditate properly/find the right practice/get enlightened – the "there" of *spirituality.*

The "*I'll be happy when...*" trap is an example most people can identify with. The core states and circumstances vary, but the basic structure of the superstition is the same:

I'll be [*core state*] when I have [*circumstance*]

It's based on an even simpler structure:

[*circumstance*] causes [*core state*]

The idea that our core states are, at least to some degree, the result of our circumstances seems so "obvious" to people that calling it into question can seem ridiculous at first.

Reality Check

I know what you may be thinking… "Are you really trying to tell me that my work doesn't actually stress me out? That my security doesn't come from money? That I don't feel love because of my partner? That I don't like going on holiday?"

Yes and no.

Your examples of your experience are real for you. I'm sure you can identify numerous circumstances where you experience certain feelings. I'm not saying you don't enjoy the things you enjoy, or that you shouldn't want the things that you want. What I'm saying is that the feelings aren't the result of the circumstances – they're coming from somewhere else entirely. And, as you start to understand where they're coming from, and how the system works, some wonderful things can start to happen.

But I'm getting ahead of myself.

These days, I experience more clarity than I ever thought possible, but I didn't get here in the way you might expect.

In brief: I grew up in an alcoholic household and started drinking heavily when I was 12 years old. By age 19, I was a scholarship engineering student and a full-blown alcoholic. The alcohol was like rocket fuel for my life – I got jobs, was promoted rapidly, and started experiencing many of the trappings of success – expense accounts, foreign travel, luxurious surroundings – but on the inside, I was slowly falling apart.

At the age of 30 I got married. A month later, her bags were packed; so I decided to stop drinking in order to save my relationship.

Oh yeah – I missed one. I'll be happy when I get a cigarette/a drink/a line of coke – the "there" of *addiction.*

That was in 1996, and I haven't had a drink since. Today I live a fulfilling life that's beyond anything I dreamed was possible for me, but how I got here is a story of struggle, frustration and heartbreak (much of which I could have avoided if I'd known what you're going to be discovering in this book).

Just to give you an idea, in the time period from 1996 to 2008...

I managed several multi-million pound projects, and struggled with a combination of fear of failure and fear of success. I got married, had two daughters and got divorced. I quit my job and built a successful training company. I got caught in an endless cycle of gaining weight and losing weight, spent countless hours talking to a Freudian psychoanalyst and participated in various addiction recovery programmes. I had numerous false horizons, thinking I'd finally "got it", only to find myself feeling like I was back where I started. By the end of 2008, I was unhappy, stressed-out and at the end of my tether. I was on the verge of giving up.

Then I was introduced to the understanding you're going to be discovering in this book. As I write, it's six years on, and they've been the best years of my life. I'm experiencing a sense of clarity, peace, security and aliveness unlike anything I've had before. And as my level of understanding has continued to increase, my relationships, results and external circumstances have been improving too.

The good news is that it can be replicated. My clients are getting similar results, including:

- less stress, more clarity and peace of mind resulting in better health, with more vibrancy and aliveness;

- fears, anxieties and limitations falling away with solutions to problems emerging more easily;

- better working relationships, and more harmony in their personal lives;

- getting more done and having more free time, with better business results, and better performance where it counts.

CLARITY   equals   Capacity   minus   Contamination

It's working for them, so it can work for you; because seeing through a misunderstanding can give you an "out of proportion" increase in the results you get. So how do you escape from this addictive, life-damaging trap? How do you start seeing through the misunderstanding, and begin to experience an enormous increase in clarity and quality of life?

keep exploring ⁜ connect with others
share your discoveries ⁜ deepen your understanding

Thought experiment: *We all fall into the "I'll be happy when..." trap from time to time. As you reflect on your life so far, what are some of the ways you're starting to realize you've been accidentally hoodwinked by this illusion until now?*

www.LittleBookOfClarity.com/chapter1

2

The Power of Insight

....

"We cannot teach people anything; we can only help them discover it within themselves."

Galileo Galilei, Astronomer, physicist and mathematician

"Don't take this the wrong way, but I get the impression that you haven't been listening very well until now…"

I thought I was a *great* listener, but my coach explained that when I was listening, it seemed like I had a lot on my mind. Listening was something I was *working* at. He said that listening in this way was OK for getting an intellectual understanding of something, but it wasn't going to help me have the clarity and insights that could make a real and lasting difference in my life.

As I reflected on it, I realized that this is how we've *all* been taught to listen. It's how we've been taught to read. It's how we've been "taught" to *learn.*

But it used to be different.

You were born a listener and learner. It's thanks to these natural abilities that you can walk and talk today. Then, we were taught to read, listen and learn for an intellectual understanding. But it's time to remember a different way to read, listen and learn…

DISTINCTION: Reading for information vs. Reading for insight

- **Reading for information:** When most people read, they're looking to verify and build upon what they know. When we read for information, we think about what we're reading *as we're reading it*, making decisions about a) whether or not we agree with it, b) where it fits into our existing cognitive structures, c) if it doesn't fit, why not?, d) whether to accept or reject it, e) if/how we're going to apply it, etc. A person who's reading for information has "something on their mind", so the mind isn't free to do what it does best – generate fresh, clear thinking.

- **Reading for insight:** When you're reading for insight, you're creating space for an "intuitive knowing" that already exists within your consciousness to emerge more fully into your awareness. Reading for insight is reading with "nothing on your mind". When you read for an insight, you put your existing conceptual models to one side and allow yourself to be *impacted* by what you're reading.

When it comes to clarity, reading for information is like drinking salt water; it just makes you more thirsty...

The magic eye

In the 1990s, evolving technology led to the creation of "magic-eye" images. At first glance, a magic-eye image looks like a repeating, two-dimensional pattern, but if you look "through" the image, with a soft-eyed, relaxed gaze, a 3D figure suddenly leaps into your awareness.

People often sat staring at the 2D images, "trying hard" to see the 3D image hidden within it, but nothing happened until they relaxed and allowed the image to emerge.

Reading for an insight is sort of like looking at a magic-eye picture. You don't really need to "think about" what you're reading – you just relax and allow yourself to be impacted by the words. The insight that can clear your mind and give you fluid, fresh thinking isn't in the words anyway; it's a capacity that's right there inside of you, "pre-loaded" into your consciousness.

Another example is music. When you listen to music you enjoy, you're not trying to decide whether you agree with it or not. You're listening to be impacted; to enjoy it and have an experience. When you're reading or listening for insight, you "get a feel" for what the person's saying, seeing beyond the written (or spoken) word to what the author's really trying to convey. You allow an intuitive knowing to emerge from within *your* consciousness (this is what's happening when you get a sudden "a-ha".)

The power of insight

To get a feel for the difference between intellectual understanding and insightful understanding, imagine a dog that's constantly chasing his tail. Now let's imagine that the dog hires you and me as consultants. We ask the dog what he needs, and he says something like this:

> "Here's what I need: First, I need more speed, because the thing I'm chasing is very fast. It always seems to be able to outrun me. Second, I need more agility, because this thing is also very nimble. Even when I creep up on it, it manages to slip away before I can catch it. Third, I need better strategy, because no matter what I do, it always seems one step ahead of me. It's almost as if it knows what I'm thinking! Finally, I need more time. I'm already working 12-hour days on this, and it just doesn't seem to be enough. So that's what I need: more speed, more agility, better strategy and more time."

You and I both know that all the dog *really* needs is to realize that it's *his own tail* he's been chasing. But if we tell him that, there are two ways the dog might respond. If he insightfully understands what we tell him, and really "gets it", then he will visibly relax, sigh and maybe even chuckle.

On the other hand, if the dog has an intellectual understanding, but doesn't have an insight, he might say something like this:

> "Right. So you're telling me that it's my tail. Got it. So I need to remember not to chase it, right? OK. So how do

I not chase my tail? Can you just take me through the process?"

If the dog says this, we know that he hasn't really understood.

The reality is that every person has this source of insight within them. You have everything you need to bring you to clarity. As you read this book for an insight, you may occasionally find yourself feeling particularly clear, calm and peaceful. That sense of clarity can be one of the signs that you're being impacted, so enjoy it when it comes and relax when it doesn't.

And what's so great about insight?

Insightful understanding often arrives suddenly, but can continue serving and informing you for years to come. It's a natural function of the mind, and has the power to make the changes that matter in your life. Insight is the key to reconnecting you with your mind's self-clearing capacity.

In fact, the primary purpose of this book is to act as a catalyst so that your own insights and realizations can bring you to clarity, guiding you and helping you make changes as you move forward. Your insights and realizations will clear up the misunderstanding that's been generating contaminated thinking and keeping you from clarity until now.

CLARITY   equals   Capacity   minus   Contamination

So I invite you to "read for an insight" as we start exploring a phenomenon that's very strange, entirely counterintuitive and still one of the most shocking things I've ever encountered…

***keep exploring ⁘ connect with others
share your discoveries ⁘ deepen your understanding***

Thought experiment: *Insight is a natural part of being alive. Sometimes, small, everyday insights end up being as profound as the big "a-has." As you think about it now, what are some of your more useful and impactful insights and a-ha moments so far?*

www.LittleBookOfClarity.com/chapter2

3

How Perception is Created

....

*"Thought creates the world then says
'I didn't do it'"*

David Bohm, Quantum physicist

"Now in a dream, our mind continuously does this... We create and perceive our world simultaneously... And our mind does this so well that we don't even know it's happening..."

These words are spoken by Leonardo DiCaprio, playing Cobb, in the film *Inception* (2010, Warner Bros. Pictures). He's explaining how dreams work, but our waking experience is generated in exactly the same way (albeit with access to a "live data feed"). To paraphrase Cobb:

> *"In your waking experience of reality, your mind continuously creates and perceives a world simultaneously... So well that you don't feel your mind doing the creating."*

The implications of this can be truly shocking. It means that 100% of your experience of the world "out there" is being generated from *inside you*, incorporating data received by the senses to a greater or lesser degree (depending on your focus of attention).

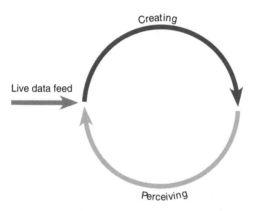

Figure 3.1   Simultaneously Creating and Perceiving

For example, a person can be asleep and dreaming that they're in the front row at a rock concert, only to wake up and discover that the music in their dream was coming from the radio next to their bed. Conversely, a person can be sitting in a business meeting, but have their focus of attention entirely absorbed by a daydream about a future holiday. Whether the data is arriving from your senses, your memories, or your imagination, the process that's generating your perceptual experience is the same.

Our experience of reality is, quite literally, created from "the stuff that dreams are made of".

Energy streams in through all our senses simultaneously as raw data, in much the same way data flows into a computer through a USB port. The mind then creates a model of "what must be out there for me to be receiving this data." This model is what's "represented" to us in consciousness.

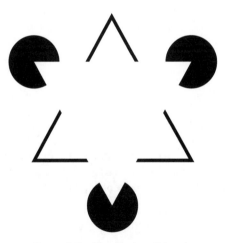

Figure 3.2   The Kanizsa Triangle

As you look at the Kanizsa Triangle, raw data from the image is intercepted by your eyes and transmitted to your brain. Your brain enhances the data, filling in the gaps and voila! The perceptual reality generated *by your mind* includes an illusory white triangle that doesn't exist in material reality.

The Pixels of Perception

As I write, I can see the words I'm typing appearing on the screen of my laptop. At any point, I can watch a video, flick through my photos, search on Google or scroll through another document. But one thing remains constant…

Everything you see on the screen is created using tiny visual building blocks called pixels.

Similarly, your experience of reality is made of the perceptual equivalent of pixels; an "energy" that I'm going to refer to as the principle of THOUGHT. (I'll use SMALL CAPS when I talk about it as a principle.)'

Thought Experiment

Look around at the environment you're in. As you notice the different elements in that environment, consider the fact that what you're seeing is actually a representation being generated by (and within) your amazing mind. Your experience of everything you can see is made of the pixels of perception: the power of THOUGHT.

Now close your eyes and remember what you were able to see in your environment. Your memory of those things is also made of THOUGHT.

Now imagine an event you're planning to enjoy in the future. This future-memory is made of THOUGHT.

When you're asleep and dreaming, your dreams are made of THOUGHT. Every experience you have in your whole life is generated using the principle of THOUGHT.

You create your own experience of reality, moment to moment, from within your consciousness, using the principle of THOUGHT…

Of course, the power of THOUGHT isn't just limited to our visual experience. While we've used the visual metaphor of pixels for explanatory purposes, our experiences of sound, smell, taste, and touch are also "constructed" from THOUGHT. So are our feelings and emotions.

THOUGHT is the reality principle…

We're born into THOUGHT, just as we're born into gravity. Our perceptual experience is 100% mind-made, using THOUGHT, the reality principle.

Reality Check

If you are scientifically-inclined you may be saying to yourself, *"Hang on a second, our perception isn't made of pixels or THOUGHT! It's made of synapses, neurons, neurochemicals and electrical currents!"*

Yes and no... Here's a way of thinking about it: The London Underground system is a complex network of tunnels, wires and tracks. While the electrical schematics of the Underground system have to be incredibly accurate, they're not very useful for finding your way from Oxford Circus to King's Cross. For that, you're better off using the Tube map, a masterpiece of simplicity and functionality.

If brain chemistry is like the electrician's schematic (accurate, but abstract and complex), then the CLARITY model is more like the tube map – simple, subjective and highly practical as you start getting the hang of it.

People are literally able to think *anything* and experience it as real: Two people watching the same movie can have two completely different experiences of it, thanks to the power of THOUGHT. Similarly, a person with a phobia uses THOUGHT to create the experience of an imminent plane crash, a spider bite or a dog attack. A person doing a job can feel inspired and energized, while the person sitting next to them feels stressed and unhappy doing *exactly the same work*. Both of them create their unique experience using THOUGHT. A person can become convinced that their partner is cheating on them, regardless of the reality of the situation. They create their perception using THOUGHT, then experience it as real. Someone can have a richly enjoyable experience, anticipating a holiday that they're planning to go on. THOUGHT is making that enjoyable experience possible, even if the holiday ends up being cancelled!

I'm not saying that we're doing this deliberately or consciously. I'm merely pointing to the capacity people have to create literally any perception using the incredible power of THOUGHT, and then experience that perception as real. This is how our experience is created, and we're using this capacity every moment of our lives.

The reason this is so relevant when it comes to escaping from the hidden hamster wheel and experiencing increasing levels of clarity is this:

100% of our experience of reality is mind-made. If a person believes they need X, Y or Z in order to feel A, B or C, then they will experience that as a perceptual reality. That's how powerful THOUGHT is.

Do you remember the structure of the superstition/ misunderstanding from Chapter One?

[circumstance] causes *[core state]*

THOUGHT has the power to bring each of the different permutations of this contaminated formula to life, and have a person experience it as an experiential reality. THOUGHT is like the special-effects department of a movie studio. Its job is to create a perceptual reality that looks, sounds and feels real, regardless of the "facts" of the situation. But we can all think of times when we "knew" something to be true, then later discovered it was an illusion, because…

Your THOUGHT-generated perceptual reality always seems real! That's its job. The sign of high-quality special effects is that you can't tell they're special effects!

And THOUGHT is the best special-effects department in the world.

So how does knowing this help us? And what does it have to do with clarity?

It turns out that the biggest obstacle to clarity is the result of a kind of "mental magic trick". Like so many magic tricks, its workings have been a secret until now. But it's time to reveal how the trick works...

---

keep exploring ❖ connect with others
share your discoveries ❖ deepen your understanding

Thought experiment: *Take a few moments to look around you. Tune in to whatever sounds you hear, and become aware of any tactile sensations you can feel. What happens when you consider the fact that 100% of the experience of your senses is being generated by THOUGHT, moment to moment? That the fabric of your experiential reality "out there" is in fact being generated by your mind?*

www.LittleBookOfClarity.com/chapter3

4

The Power of Principles

....

*"Misdirection is the art of initiating
a train of thought in the mind
of the spectator."*

Alan Alan, Escapologist and illusionist

**"It seems as though you've been thinking your happiness,
security and general OK-ness is dependent on you achieving your goals…"**

"Yes… Obviously!" I replied. I'd just finished explaining to one
of my mentors why it was so vitally important that I achieve a
particular objective.

"That means you don't understand where your security and well-being come from," he told me. "Your happiness, security and OK-ness don't come from outside you, so they're not vulnerable to anything outside you."

I'd fallen for a trick that's been bedevilling people for thousands of years. I'd been fooled into thinking my happiness and well-being were dependent on my circumstances.

DISTINCTION: Outside-in vs. Inside-out

- **Inside-out:** We're always living in the feeling of the principle of THOUGHT taking form in the moment. None of our *experience* is coming from anywhere other than THOUGHT. Our experience of life is less like looking through the viewfinder of a camera, and more like wearing a pair of virtual reality goggles. Data streams in through our senses, and we weave it into an experiential reality from the **inside-out** using the principle of THOUGHT.

- **Outside-in:** Due to a trick of the mind, it often *appears* as though we're feeling something *other than* the principle of THOUGHT taking form in the moment; like our experience is being created from the **outside-in**. This illusion can be very compelling, but it *never* works that way.

History is full of these illusions and false appearances:

- **Flat earth vs. Spherical earth:** People used to believe the earth was flat, because that's how it looked to them. But it was never flat; it was always spherical, with some bulging. It's spherical 100% of the time, even when it looks like it isn't.

- **Geo-centric vs. Solar-centric:** People used to believe the sun went round the earth, because that's how it looked to them. But the sun never went round the earth; the earth always went round the sun. The earth goes round the sun 100% of the time, even when it looks like it doesn't.

Our experience is being generated from the inside-out, 100% of the time, even when it looks like it isn't. There are two basic mistakes of attribution that people tend to make because of the outside-in misunderstanding:

Mistake #1 – We tend to mistakenly attribute our fulfilling, enjoyable experiences to something *other than* the principle of THOUGHT. But our fulfilling, enjoyable, desirable feelings are THOUGHT-generated; they only ever come from within us.

Examples:

- I'll be successful once I get the promotion.
- I'm secure because I've got money in the bank.
- I'll have a sense of freedom once I quit my job.
- I'm confident and outgoing because of my upbringing.

Our feelings, states and emotions can't possibly come from any-where other than THOUGHT, because our experience is mind-made.

We live in an "inside-out" world, and the experiences we enjoy only ever come from within us. Period.

Mistake #2 – We tend to mistakenly attribute our uneasy, unpleasant feelings to something *other than* the principle of THOUGHT taking form in the moment. Our uneasy, unpleasant, agitated feelings are THOUGHT-generated; they only ever come from within us.

Examples:

- I feel anxious about the job interview.
- I'd be devastated if you left me.
- I'm afraid of failure.
- I'm shy because of my upbringing.

As you can see, these two mistakes are the same misunderstanding. The outside-in misunderstanding is the *source* of contaminated thinking. I'm not saying that job interviews, promotions, money and upbringings don't exist; I'm just saying that none of our feelings come from them. 100% of our experience of interviews, promotions, money and upbringings comes from within us – we're always living in the experience of the principle of THOUGHT taking form, moment to moment.

Imagine a snow-globe that's been vigorously shaken. The snow fills the entire globe, obscuring everything else. But the moment you set the snow-globe down, the snow starts to settle, and the liquid clears. Contaminated thinking is like the snow in the snow-globe; plentiful and impenetrable, but with no meaningful substance.

Clarity is like the liquid in a snow-globe. It's always there, behind the scenes, ready to start emerging the moment you insightfully see the inside-out nature of reality; the realization that you're feeling the principle of Thought taking form in the moment...

CLARITY equals **Capacity** minus **Contamination**

And that THOUGHT-generated experiential reality is "brought to life" by the principles behind clarity.

The principles behind clarity

In 1974, a Scottish welder named Sydney Banks had a sudden, transformational insight into the nature of experience. He insight-fully saw that our experience of life is generated from psychological principles; principles as fundamental and constant as gravity. You can think of these principles as the source of (and basis for) 100% of our subjective experience of life.

THOUGHT: The reality principle
People think. The principle of THOUGHT refers to our innate capacity to generate a perceptual reality; an outer and inner world that we

can see, hear, feel, taste and smell. This principle is also the source of the countless thoughts and perceptions that arise in the course of a day.

CONSCIOUSNESS: The experience principle
People are aware. The principle of CONSCIOUSNESS refers to our capacity to have an experience; it brings our THOUGHT-generated experiential reality to life.

MIND: The power principle
People are alive. The principle of MIND is the "intelligent energy" that shows up in all aspects of the natural world. MIND is the "power-source" behind life. Various cultures and fields have different names for this power: life force, universal energy, chi, nature, the great spirit, God, the no-thing, evolution, random chance, etc. You can think of it in whatever way makes sense to you.

So what's the point of learning about principles?

Principles are a source of massive leverage. When you understand the principles behind something, it increases your power exponentially. For example...

The principles of flight

For thousands of years, people struggled with the mystery of flight. While people saw birds and insects flying, they didn't understand the principles that made flight possible. Then, the Wright brothers discovered the principles of aeronautics. In December 1903 they achieved the first manned, machine-powered flight. In the century since, the world of aeronautics has achieved extraordinary feats. Discovering the principles of aeronautics gave people massive leverage to create things that couldn't even be *dreamt* of previously.

Even a rudimentary awareness of principles has implications for your behaviour. While you may only have a basic understanding of germ theory, it's likely that you've learned to wash your hands regularly, cover your mouth when you cough and are careful when handling anything you think is a significant source of germs and bacteria.

The CLARITY® model is a business-friendly coding of the principles behind clarity, and the implications of those principles. As you continue getting a deeper understanding of these principles, you'll start experiencing a gentle yet powerful transformation, with more clarity, resilience and well-being. And why does insightful understanding of these principles make such an impact in people's lives?

Clarity of understanding leads to clarity of thought...

The outside-in misunderstanding – the false assumption that we're feeling something *other than* THOUGHT in the moment – is the only thing that ever keeps us from clarity. Clear up the misunderstanding, and the mind clears.

CLARITY   equals   **Capacity**   minus   **Contamination**

The factory settings

Clarity, resilience and peace of mind are the default setting for people; our true nature. They are our natural state when our minds are clear and free from contaminated thinking. As you continue deepening your understanding of these principles, you'll start experiencing the "default settings" more of the time. These default settings are the "deep drivers" behind individual and business success.

Deep Driver	What it drives...
Clarity: A clear mind, free from superstitious thinking, fully present and in the moment, with the levels of performance, satisfaction and enjoyment that brings.	• High performance • Effective leadership • Presence • Insight • Confidence • Timely decision making • Detecting opportunities • Competitive advantage • Rapid response to change • Dealing with complexity • Productivity • Reduced stress • Increased focus

Deep Driver	What it drives...
Direction: A sense of direction, purpose and motivation, free from urgency and undue pressure.	• Authentic leadership • Shared vision and purpose • Focus of resources • Employee engagement • Strategic planning • Brand clarity and passion • Sustainability • Resolves uncertainty • Shared goals • Motivation
Resilience: A strong sense of inner resilience, security and trust in yourself and your world.	• Thriving through uncertainty • Rapid recovery from setbacks • Dealing with change • Responsiveness and flexibility • Confident delivery • Agility and staying power • Mental fitness/toughness
Creativity: A reliable source of creativity and insight for innovating and solving problems.	• Soft and hard innovation • Problem-solving • Disruptive strategy • Blue ocean strategy • Product and service design • Customer delight • Market leadership • Brand narrative • Opportunity creation

Deep Driver	What it drives...
Connection: Warm, genuine connections with other people, leading to stronger relationships with clients, colleagues, friends, family-members and lovers.	• Understanding customer needs • Service culture • Employee engagement • Effective meetings • Productive, agile teams • Collaborative solutions • Contribution and caring • Sustainability • Social marketing • Effective communication • Effective listening • Persuasion and influence • Word of mouth/referrals • Brand loyalty
Authenticity: The freedom to be who you are, speak your truth and do what you believe to be right.	• Authentic leadership • Integrity • Transparency • Customer loyalty • Employee engagement • Brand clarity and passion • Trust and credibility • Raving fans • Differentiation

Deep Driver	What it drives...
Intuition: Alignment with your intuition and inner wisdom, your internal guidance system.	• Effective decision making • Opportunity spotting • Disruptive offerings • Blue ocean strategy • Market leadership • Soft and hard innovation • Product and service design • Competitive advantage • Sustainability
Presence: Present, aware and available to the moment, connected with your mind, your body and the world around you.	• Influencing others • Charismatic leadership • Clear view of reality • Enhanced awareness • Enhanced forecasting • Trend-detection • Opportunity spotting • Natural attractiveness • Embodied learning

Context-sensitive

The mind is context-sensitive. The CLARITY® model points to an extraordinary "intelligence" capable of giving you what you need when you need it. The mindset that's most practical and useful for a job interview isn't necessarily the one that will give you the richest experience of sharing a sunset with your lover. The mindset that's most effective when coming up with a solution to a serious business problem isn't necessarily the one that will help you deliver the goods when you're delivering an inspirational speech to rally the troops.

The more deeply you *understand* the principles behind clarity, the more you get to benefit from the *implications* of these principles.

Even when we know about them, we all sometimes lose sight of the fact that principles are creating our experience of life. We get caught up in our thinking and slip into the outside-in illusion. Fortunately, there's a brilliant system we've each got to let you know when that's happened, and point you back in the direction of clarity...

---

keep exploring ❖ connect with others
share your discoveries ❖ deepen your understanding

Thought experiment: *I invite you to open to the possibility that the qualities people prize most highly (clarity, creativity, love, peace, presence and freedom, to name just a few) are traits you already possess. How surprised would you be if you were to suddenly realize these qualities are your natural state when there's nothing else in the way?*

www.LittleBookOfClarity.com/chapter4

5

The Psychological Immune System

....

"The major problems in the world are the result of the difference between how nature works and the way people think."

Gregory Bateson, Epistemologist

"You're feeling your thinking, not what you're thinking about..."

My friend looked bemused by my statement. He wanted me to cure his fear of flying, so I started by asking how he knew when to start becoming afraid, and how he knew when to stop. He told me that it usually started a week before his flight, and dissipated 20 or 30 minutes after takeoff.

"I've got some great news for you", I told him. *"You're not afraid of flying!"*

"I'm not?" he asked in surprise.

"*No*", I replied. "*You have fearful **thinking** around flying.*"

"*Isn't that the same thing?*" he responded, dubiously.

"*No, it isn't the same thing*", I said. "*You're feeling your **thinking**, not what you're thinking **about**...*"

People are notoriously bad at predicting their felt response to imagined scenarios. David is sure he'll fall apart if he gets made redundant, but it turns out to be one of the best things that's ever happened to him. Jennifer is convinced that her job is the source of all her woes, but when she gets a new one, her woes come along for the ride. Michael is excited about starting a business, sure he's going to love it, but he ends up struggling with stress and disillusionment. Susan has massive self-doubt but starts a new venture anyway. As she begins making progress, she blossoms and thrives.

And why are we so bad at these predictions?

Because we're living in the feeling of the principle of THOUGHT taking form *in the moment*; not in the feeling of what we're thinking *about*.

The tip of the iceberg

The portion of an iceberg that's visible above the water's surface typically only represents 11% of the iceberg's total volume. Looking at the tip doesn't tell you anything about the shape of the submerged portion of the iceberg.

Our THOUGHT-generated perceptual reality is like an iceberg...

We live in a THOUGHT-generated experiential reality; 100% of our experience is coming from the principle of THOUGHT taking form in the moment. But the individual thoughts that we notice going through our minds (i.e. what we're thinking *about*) are like the tip of the iceberg; they only comprise a tiny portion of the thinking that's creating our experience of the moment. Like the submerged portion of the iceberg, the majority of our thinking is invisible.

So how do you know what's in the invisible portion of your thinking? Your feelings. Feeling and thinking are like two sides of the same coin. Your feelings are the visible face of your (invisible) thinking.

So what does this have to do with clarity?

When we believe we're feeling something *other than* the principle of THOUGHT taking form, our minds fill up and speed up. The more contaminated thinking is in our minds, the less clarity we experience. The less contaminated thinking is in our minds, the more clarity we experience. When you're experiencing a high

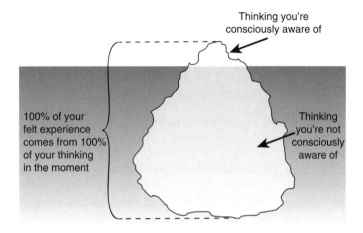

Thinking you're
consciously aware of

100% of your
felt experience
comes from 100%
of your thinking
in the moment

Thinking
you're not
consciously
aware of

Figure 5.1   The Thinking/Feeling iceberg

degree of clarity, you're not thinking about anything; you've got nothing on your mind. This is sometimes described as "flow".

Fearful thinking

If flying was genuinely the cause of my friend's anxiety, he would be at his most frightened when the plane was in the air, and it wouldn't start diminishing until after the plane had landed. The fact that he spent the major portion of the flight feeling fine meant that he wasn't afraid of flying; he was experiencing something else entirely.

The pain withdrawal reflex is an involuntary response that moves your body (or part of your body) away from a source of pain.

If you've ever accidentally touched a candle flame or a hot stove, you've experienced the pain withdrawal reflex. While the response is involuntary (i.e. not under your conscious control), it's still mediated by THOUGHT. A person who is under the influence of drink or drugs will not always exhibit the response, and people can actually be conditioned to override it.

Your psychological immune system

Just as we each receive pain signals to let us know when our physical well-being is under threat, we also receive signals that "wake us up" when our heads are filling up with contaminated thinking.

The mental equivalent of the pain withdrawal reflex is most clearly exhibited in children under five years old. Toddlers can go from excruciating mental torment one minute to laughing and giggling the next. Even the most extreme tantrum doesn't last for long in the big scheme of things; certainly not as long as most adults' bouts of contaminated thinking.

A little child will only go so far into painful thinking, and only stay there so long before the "mental pain withdrawal reflex" kicks in and guides them back to clarity. The psychological immune system takes care of their mental well-being just as the physical immune system takes care of their physical well-being. So why isn't this response so obvious in teenagers and adults?

People can be conditioned to override it…

The natural system we have for guiding us out of painful contaminated thinking gets overridden by our conditioning. So if we've been conditioned out of it, how do we "wake up" when we're lost in thought?

We are all born with a fully functioning psychological immune system; mentally ill infants are few and far between. But as we grow up, we get conditioned into thought-habits of our family and our culture; thought-habits that include the outside-in misunderstanding. Some people are less conditioned by it than others; you probably know people who seem to be unusually resilient and philosophical in the face of hardship and crisis, just as you know others who seem to fall apart at the slightest provocation. The variable is this:

People who seem to fall apart at the slightest provocation are convinced that their thinking is real. People who are resilient and resourceful in the face of hardship and crisis intuitively know their thinking is an illusion...

So how do you begin to "see through" this conditioning? Insightful understanding. As you continue reading this book and deepening your understanding of the principles behind clarity, you'll start to notice stale habits of contaminated thinking dropping away, and clarity emerging to take their place.

CLARITY   equals   **Capacity**   minus   **Contamination**

Rumble strips

On motorways, highways and autobahns all over the world, rumble strips along the side of the road alert drivers who are travelling too near the edge. The signal is simple and well understood: they've started to go off-track. The moment a driver starts feeling the rumble, they correct their course easily.

We all drift off the road into contaminated thinking; it's part of our experience. But as you start to see through the outside-in misunderstanding, something changes. At some point when you start to go off track, it will occur to you that your feelings are coming from THOUGHT taking form in the moment. This is the start of your psychological immune system's self-correcting process. You don't need to do anything to help it along; the process of self-correction is an automatic function of your mind.

And everyone has it!

So if everyone has this powerful and elegant system built into them, why do so many people spend so much of their time riding on the rumble strips? If everyone's got this natural ability to find their clarity and wisdom, why is there so much stress, pressure and conflict? So much crime, divorce, addiction and war? If everyone has an innate guidance system for keeping them on track, why does it so often seem like they're not using it?

keep exploring ❖ connect with others
share your discoveries ❖ deepen your understanding

Thought experiment: *"The major problems in the world are the result of the difference between how nature works and the way people think." Take a moment or two to reflect on Gregory Bateson's statement. By definition, it must apply to the problems of business, of relationships, of our personal struggles. Could it really be this simple?*

www.LittleBookOfClarity.com/chapter5

6

Habitual Thought Patterns

....

"What the thinker thinks, the prover proves."

Leonard Orr, Writer and philosopher

"It took a long time for my thinking to get this messed up, so it's going to take a long time for it to get sorted out…"

This simple piece of "received wisdom" echoes through the world of addiction-recovery, and it reveals a basic confusion about the mind: People tend to think, speak and act as though their *thoughts* have the same qualities as the material world. We all write down phone numbers, notes and to-do lists; because we recognize that our thoughts are fleeting and ephemeral. Yet we don't seem to remember that fact in other areas of our lives. Consider the following statements:

- "The company's *issues* are really *deep-rooted*. They won't be easy to *resolve*."
- "This is a really *big problem*. It's going to be *tough* for our team to *sort it out*."

These statements each contain false implications that arise from attributing material-world qualities to thoughts. For instance:

- "It took *a long time* for my thinking to get this *messed up*, so it's going to take *a long time* for it to get *sorted out*."

False implications: Messy thinking is like a messy office or a garden that hasn't been cared for. The more time that elapses as it gets messy, the more time (and effort) it's going to take to sort it out. Like some enormous warehouse full of stuff, the more time spent on making it messy, the longer it takes to tidy it up.

Reality: THOUGHT is a creative energy, and the THOUGHT-forms we create using it have no substance; they're literally made of "the stuff that dreams are made of." Have you ever noticed how fleeting dreams can be? How one minute you're experiencing a rich dreamscape, and the next minute you're wide awake and having trouble remembering what the dream was about? The dream is so fleeting because it's made of THOUGHT. And your thinking is made of the same thing. It can change instantly the moment you have an insight. Time is a function of the material world, but the principle of Thought isn't subject to the laws of the material world. People can experience a moment of clarity, and see a situation (or their lives) change in a matter of moments.

Medication time... medication time...

I started drinking alcohol when I was 12 years old. By the time I was 20, I was what's referred to as a "high-functioning alcoholic". I loved the feeling of peace, freedom and aliveness that alcohol seemed to give me. But I was deeply troubled by the effects it had on my life, and the lives of those around me. I tried to control my drinking, but every attempt at control eventually resulted in greater chaos. By the time I was 30, I was done. I had a moment of clarity, and decided to stop drinking. But things went from bad to worse. After nine months without a drink, I was depressed and suicidal. My habitual patterns of contaminated thinking were robbing my life of any sense of peace, joy or aliveness. So I decided to get help.

Over the past 18 years, I've come to see the alcoholic's drinking, the drug addict's using, and every other addict's seemingly pathological behaviour, as an example of medicating. And what is the addict trying to medicate?

Habitual patterns of contaminated thinking that seem like they're a material reality; like there's more to them than Thought.

The addict's use of drink/drugs/sex/shopping/gambling is an "intervention" that offers temporary relief from their contaminated thinking, and the painful feelings that often accompany it. Similarly, many of the behavioural problems people experience are the result of an attempt to medicate agitated feelings that *look* like they're coming from something *other than* THOUGHT taking form in the moment.

Contaminated thinking (and the feelings that accompany it) is all that ever stands between us and the high levels of clarity, security and peace of mind we all have within us.

CLARITY   equals   Capacity   minus   Contamination

The river still flows

Imagine a river that starts to cool as winter comes. As the temperature falls, ice crystals begin to form along the riverbanks. As it keeps getting colder, the crystals start forming small blocks of ice that break free of the banks and flow down the river. At various points the blocks of ice cluster together, and the river begins to freeze over. Eventually, the surface of the river is a solid sheet of ice. But all the while, just beneath the surface, the river still flows.

Our habits of contaminated thinking are like a thin layer of ice on the surface of the river; the only thing that ever stands in the way of clarity, and a rich experience of life. But beneath that seemingly solid mass, the river still flows. Just as the ice was created from flowing water, our habits of contaminated thinking are created from THOUGHT, the formless energy behind our experience of life.

And behind all our contaminated thinking, the endless river of THOUGHT is still flowing, carrying the powerful resources of innate clarity, resilience and well-being to the surface of our awareness; bringing fresh new thinking to solve our problems and create new possibilities.

When we're locked in a mind-made prison of habitual thoughts, it seems ludicrous to think that freedom could be so nearby. At least, until you realize who has the key...

---

keep exploring ∴ connect with others
share your discoveries ∴ deepen your understanding

Thought experiment: *Is it possible that many of the things you've been experiencing as problems until now are a reflection of the mistaken belief that your thinking was real?*

www.LittleBookOfClarity.com/chapter6

7

Stress: The Source and the Solution

....

"You're always living in the feeling of your thinking."

Keith Blevens PhD, Clinical psychologist

"What are you looking for?"

The time was 2 a.m. The policeman had just walked round the corner to find an intoxicated-looking man on his hands and knees, searching frantically beneath a streetlight.

"I'm looking for my key", the man slurred.

"Where did you lose it?" the officer inquired.

"I dropped it in the long grass on a vacant lot, a couple of blocks away", said the man, still searching.

"Then why are you looking here?" asked the puzzled cop.

The man rolled his eyes and said, *"Because the light's better here."*

The man's mistake in this Sufi joke is so obvious as to be ridiculous, but there are times when we are all that drunken seeker. Each of us is searching under a streetlight for the key that isn't there when we're looking to the outside for the security/resilience/wellbeing/creativity/confidence/connection/fulfilment/success we desire.

The source of stress

So what does this have to do with stress? Here's what:

The true source of stress is the mistaken belief that we're feeling something other than the principle of THOUGHT taking form in the moment...

... that we're at the mercy of something other than our moment-to-moment thinking; a world "out there" in space or time with power over how we feel...

THOUGHT is the formless energy that creates the form of our moment-to-moment experience. Just as sand can be used to make any kind of sandcastle or sand sculpture, THOUGHT can create any kind of perceptual form. THOUGHT creates an experiential reality in an instant; we're in it before we realize THOUGHT has anything to do with it.

Misdirection is the initiation of a train of thought based on a false assumption. The moment we believe our felt experience is coming from something *other than* the principle of THOUGHT taking form in the moment, we've accepted a false assumption and climbed aboard. This is the inevitable result of believing that thinking and feeling are separate; they're not. Thinking and feeling are two sides of the same coin. Which means...

We're never stressed out about what we believe we're stressed out about...

We're only ever stressed out because we believe we're feeling something other than the principle of THOUGHT taking form in the moment...

The belief that we're feeling something other than our thinking turns us into victims. Some people respond to that by retreating, defending or manipulating, while others come out fighting; either way, they're responding to an illusion. Of course, this doesn't just apply to stress; everything from worry and anxiety to anger and rage can be the result of this subtle but catastrophic misdirection.

And, strange as it may seem, it can also apply to pleasant experiences. The idea that our fun/happy/enjoyable/exciting/loving feelings are coming from something other than THOUGHT in the moment is equally misguided; it just doesn't work that way.

We're always and only feeling the principle of THOUGHT taking form in the moment. Period. It only works one way. Even when it looks *like we're feeling something other than* THOUGHT *in the moment, it still only works one way...*

The light's better here

We innocently look in the tangible (but illusory) world of form for our clarity, well-being, security and success because the light's so much better here. But you can never find something where it isn't, no matter how hard you look. Our experience of the world of form is an illusion: an often-practical one, but an illusion nevertheless.

Your felt experience doesn't come from the illusion... Your felt experience comes from what's creating *the illusion...*

It comes from the principles that are creating 100% of your experience of reality...

Because the intellect is a form-manipulation system, and cannot conceive of something "formless", we need to use metaphors to point to it. The words THOUGHT, CONSCIOUSNESS and MIND are themselves metaphors that point to the formless energy creating our experience of life.

As we go through life, we experience the form of our inner and outer worlds. The formless principles behind clarity are what's creating that experience.

The solution to stress

When we're lost in contaminated thinking, we tend to be obsessed with the "forms" of life. But, as clarity emerges, the forms don't appear to be important in the same way. Athletes often report that when they're in the zone, it seems as though, on the one hand, it doesn't matter whether they win or lose and, on the other hand, they're going to give it all they've got.

This doesn't even make *sense* as an intellectual construct, but as clarity emerges, it becomes self-evident. We naturally tend to be less concerned with the form of our thinking, and more aligned with what's creating it; a direction that's accompanied by a deeper felt experience of life, and a sense of well-being.

While we don't all have the words to describe it, every one of us has experienced it. For one person it may be when they're walking through the woods or looking out at the waves on the ocean; for another person it may be when they're deeply involved in an activity like dancing or running. But they all share something in common...

When we have clarity and peace of mind, it's not personal. We don't tend to be caught up in the form of our contaminated, "it's all about me", thinking. Situations which may have seemed infuriating are suddenly no longer an issue. We "just know" that things will turn out alright.

This deeper, more connected sense is a signal that you're look-ing away from the *form* of your thoughts, and are more aligned with what's creating them; the formless principles of THOUGHT, CONSCIOUSNESS and MIND. An understanding of the formless can be seen in a variety of domains, and goes by many names:

- The no-thing (Buddhism)
- The implicate order (Bohmian physics)
- Life energy (some biologists)
- Spirit (spirituality)
- The great spirit (North American Indians)

Many names, but one direction; looking beyond our experience of the form of life to where that experience is coming from.

So what's the "solution" to stress? Insightful understanding of the inside-out nature of life. The moment we insightfully see that 100% of our feeling is coming from THOUGHT in the moment (and not from anything other than that), feelings of stress start diminishing and clarity starts emerging. This doesn't make us "immune" to stress – we still get hoodwinked by contaminated thinking from time to time. But as you continue exploring the principles behind clarity, you'll begin to notice your stress levels decreasing in general, and that you have a very different response to many things which used to "stress you out".

CLARITY equals Capacity minus Contamination

And why is "insightful understanding" likely to succeed in a world where the prevailing psychological (non)paradigm identifies an increasing number of different mental disorders every year? Where governments throw their hands up in despair at the rise in addictions, depression and stress? Where businesses are paralyzed in the face of disruptive competitors and increasing complexity? Where individuals battle with attention-poverty, time-scarcity and information-overload?

The answer to all these questions is to be found in a newly discovered leverage point for transformation...

---

keep exploring ∻ *connect with others*
share your discoveries ∻ *deepen your understanding*

Thought experiment: *What would it mean to you (and for you) if you were to suddenly realize that 100% of your felt experience is coming from THOUGHT taking form in the moment? That 0% of your feeling is coming from anywhere other than THOUGHT?*

www.LittleBookOfClarity.com/chapter7

8

The Ultimate Leverage Point

....

"The historian of science may be tempted to exclaim that when paradigms change, the world itself changes with them."

Thomas Kuhn, Physicist, historian
and philosopher of science

**"Pay no attention to that man behind the curtain. Go –
before I lose my temper! The Great and Powerful Oz has
spoken…"**

When I was a little boy, I loved the film *The Wizard of Oz*, but I
was frightened of the Wicked Witch of the West and her flying
monkeys. On some level, I didn't understand that those monkeys

were just people in costumes, and couldn't escape from the television screen.

I didn't understand the nature of film.

Hallucinations

One of my first ever coaching clients had a dog phobia. I asked her *"How do you know when to get frightened?"* Her head shot back, and she said *"As soon as I see the gnashing jaws"*, while using her hands to mimic a dog snapping at her face. When she saw a dog, even if it was 50 feet away and on a lead, she would generate this frightening hallucination and respond accordingly.

She was responding to a THOUGHT-generated illusion as though it was a material reality.

It's easy to dismiss my dog-phobic client's fear as "irrational", but each of us gets hypnotized by the same order of illusion on a daily basis. Whether a person is worrying or daydreaming; stressing out because they're stuck in traffic or getting excited about a date they're going on later; they're experiencing a THOUGHT-generated perceptual reality.

So what has this got to do with clarity?

> *Increasing clarity is the inevitable result of a transformation in your* understanding *of how life works…*

When it comes to people changing, there are four "levels" where a person can get leverage.

Level 1 – Material reality

The material world is bound by certain laws, such as gravity. If a person drops a brick on their foot, it will likely do some damage. If a person exercises regularly, their muscles will get stronger.

Level 2 – The content of thinking (i.e. what you're thinking about)

Sigmund Freud popularized the idea that the *content* of a person's memories "caused" their current experience. Making changes at this level is like changing the content of a movie (or making up stories about the impact of movies you watched in the past).

Level 3 – The structure of thinking

The originators of neuro-linguistic programming (NLP) came to the conclusion that the *structure* of a person's thinking plays a significant role in shaping their experience. Making changes at the level of structure is like playing with the shot selection, camera angles and soundtrack in a film.

Level 4 – The nature of THOUGHT

THOUGHT creates our multi-sensory "picture" of reality; our experience of the world is created "from the inside-out" via the principles of MIND, THOUGHT and CONSCIOUSNESS. Insightfully understanding what's *behind* the scenes of our experience (i.e. seeing the nature of THOUGHT) can lead to a profound transformation, increasing clarity, security and peace of mind. People often experience a significant reduction in stress, and an increase in their sense of resiliency, regardless of external circumstances. Longstanding problems and issues often disappear without being "worked on".

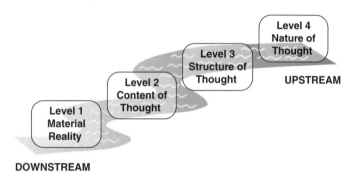

DOWNSTREAM

Figure 8.1   The Four levels of Psychological leverage

When it comes to films, the most powerful shift a person can experience is a shift in understanding. Once a person insightfully understands the nature of films, they can watch scenes which would previously have put them in fear for their lives.

Until a person understands the nature of films, it can really seem like those flying monkeys are going to come out of the screen and get them.

But they won't. Ever. Because that's not the nature of films. It doesn't work that way.

Until a person understands the nature of movies, the best they can do is keep reminding themselves that *"It's just a movie, it's just a movie..."* Once a person insightfully understands the nature of movies, they don't have to do anything. No further intervention is necessary. They can still be deeply affected by a film, but they know that their well-being isn't at risk.

> *Until a person understands the nature of THOUGHT, intervention at the level of content or structure seems to make sense. As you begin to understand the nature of THOUGHT, intervention at the level of content or structure starts losing its appeal...*

The flying monkeys can't get out of the screen. Ever...

DISTINCTION: Externally-corrected vs. Self-correcting

- **Externally-corrected:** A system that needs an external agent to diagnose problems, then take action to put them right, can be referred to as externally-corrected. If a car breaks down, it won't fix itself.

- **Self-correcting:** A self-correcting system requires no external intervention; it just needs the right conditions and enough time to resolve any issues. The primary condition required for a self-correcting system to find its way back to balance is simple: an absence of external interference.

The CLARITY® model is grounded in "implication-based learning". It focuses on helping a client to insightfully understand the nature of THOUGHT, and the principles behind how our experience is created. As such, there is no need for external-correction.

Like understanding the nature of film, as soon as a person gets an insight into the nature of THOUGHT, their entire experience of reality starts to change. They start living in the implications of that understanding. Certified Clarity® coaches, consultants and practitioners work with clients to help them get an insight into the nature of THOUGHT, secure in the knowledge that the client really does have everything they need to self-correct; to find clarity, solve their problems, and create the results that matter to them.

There's a huge difference between intervening in an existing perceptual reality, versus looking upstream at what's *creating* that perceptual reality. If a person doesn't understand that they're feeling the principle of THOUGHT taking form in the moment, they'll accept what their perception has to tell them about those feelings.

THOUGHT creates the world then says "I didn't do it"...

On the other hand, the moment a person starts to insightfully understand the *nature* of THOUGHT, they experience a freedom in relation to the experiential reality it's generating. This represents a new paradigm for our understanding of the mind.

The power of a paradigm

In his groundbreaking book, *The Structure of Scientific Revolutions*, Thomas Kuhn explains that every scientific field has a pre-paradigm phase, during which the field has no shared basis or foundation to build upon. During this time, the field is beset by anomalies, with scientists working hard to explain them. Then, at a certain point, a paradigm emerges. Now the field has a shared foundation; a basis for further experiment and exploration. A new paradigm often results from the discovery of principles. For instance, Newton's discovery of the principle of gravity (and his resulting "law of universal gravitation") established a new paradigm for physics; a foundation on which subsequent work was based. Einstein's work on relativity established a further paradigm. Schrodinger's and Bohr's work on quantum physics established yet another, and so on.

The field of psychology has been in its pre-paradigm phase until now. This explains the plethora of (often conflicting) theories, techniques and models. It also explains the many thousands of books published each year on personal development, business psychology and leadership models.

What the discovery of the principles behind clarity makes possible is the realization of a single paradigm; a worldview underlying the theories and methodology of all aspects of psychology. When we shift from the pre-paradigm phase to the acceptance of a single paradigm, it has a profound impact. Consider the following examples:

The Solar System

In the pre-paradigm phase, people believed planet earth was the centre of the universe. Calendars were inaccurate, and had to be adjusted occasionally to catch up. There was difficulty in predicting movement of planets. In the post-paradigm phase, people know that the sun is the centre of the solar system. Calendars are accurate, and there is greater ability to predict movement of planets, etc.

Germ Theory

In the pre-paradigm phase, people believed disease and illness was caused by a range of factors including miasmas and atmospheres. Doctors innocently made matters worse, spreading and exacerbating illness due to misunderstanding. In the post-paradigm phase, there is near-universal awareness of germ theory. Individuals take sensible precautions to avoid illness, and doctors and nurses scrub up, sterilize instruments, etc. All of this results in a massive reduction in illness, near-eradication of many diseases, and an unprecedented 30-year increase in the average lifespan.

Flight

In the pre-paradigm phase, there were countless attempts to create a manned, powered aircraft, using a variety of ingenious methods, with not a single successful flight. In the post-paradigm phase, we have manned aircraft, international jet travel, and the emergence of package holidays.

The flat-earth theory, the geo-centric universe and the miasma model are now seen as quaint historical curiosities. The principled, single-paradigm model of psychology (as summed up by the statement "100% of our feeling is arising from the principle of THOUGHT taking form in the moment") puts numerous other psychological models and theories to rest.

I've seen profound transformations in my clients as they get an understanding of the nature of THOUGHT. People start making progress on dreams that had seemed impossible until now. Business teams start working together and delivering results more creatively and effectively than ever before. Conflicts get resolved, and relationships get back on track. Clarity increases and performance improves. People suddenly discover that they've got more time in the day, as they spend less and less time in contaminated thinking. Individuals often start experiencing a quality of life and peace of mind unlike anything they've experienced until now.

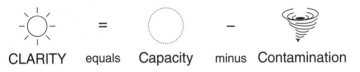

CLARITY   equals   Capacity   minus   Contamination

And what's the source of the kind of clarity/creativity/presence/authenticity/motivation/connection/resilience/peace of mind and enjoyment of life most people yearn for?

I'll give you a hint: You've already got it…

keep exploring ⁘ connect with others
share your discoveries ⁘ deepen your understanding

Thought experiment: *One of the more profound implications of the principles behind clarity is this: you don't need to control, monitor or manage your thinking. What happens when you stop for a moment and deeply consider that?*

www.LittleBookOfClarity.com/chapter8

PART TWO

The Deep Drivers

9

Innate Clarity and Peace of Mind

....

"We don't know who discovered water, but we know it wasn't the fish."

Marshall McLuhan, Media theorist

"I don't need you to change. And I don't need anything from you. Whether you believe it or not, you don't need to do a thing…"

I burst into tears.

The year was 2004, and I'd just travelled several hundred miles to have a session with a coach. When I arrived, I explained that I really needed a breakthrough, and was worried that if I didn't "get it right", my time and money would be wasted, and I would be no further forward. Worse still, I would be stuck in the stress and dis-ease that had me come to him in the first place.

He told me I didn't need to do *anything*, and I burst into tears. And as I sat there with tears streaming down my face, I started to feel more peaceful. We sat and talked for three hours, and by the time we were finished, I felt better than I had in ages. And I was so happy that I was feeling better, I didn't think to ask some obvious questions...

1   Where do the deep, rich, profound feelings in life come from?

2   Where do they go when you're not aware of them?

3   What are the factors determining whether you're aware of them or not?

Your understanding of how life works

Your understanding of how life works has more influence than *any other factor* over your experience of life, and the results you get. We each behave in accordance with what makes sense to us:

- In Aztec culture, it "made sense" to sacrifice people to the gods in order to keep the community thriving.

- In England in the 1850s, it "made sense" to dump raw sewage into the River Thames and carry small bunches of flowers to protect against illness.

- In Japanese culture, it "makes sense" for many people to work 12 hours a day, 6 days a week, for months or even years on end (the Japanese even have a word, karōshi, which means literally "death from overwork").

In 2004, my understanding of "how life works" dictated that all feelings and states could be recreated, accessed and utilized by manipulating a person's body, their breathing, and their thinking patterns. Mental-emotional states were something a person "chose", "got into", and "managed".

But, as you start to understand the principles behind clarity more clearly, the idea of managing your states shows a misunderstanding of what states, feelings and emotions are; the idea of "state control" stops making sense.

You have innate clarity and peace of mind

Clarity and peace of mind are the "default position" for people – the factory settings. While these are context-sensitive – they can show up differently depending on the situation – they're the baseline for a person when there's nothing else in the way. And what gets in the way? Contaminated thinking.

Like a football being held underwater, as soon as you let go, it rises to the surface. And like the grass pressing up through the cracks in a city pavement, your resilience and clarity is always doing its best to find its way through the paving slabs of your contaminated thinking...

Clarity is the small child's standard setting. Up to the age of around four years old, children return easily to the default setting of their clarity and well-being. While they often get upset, they don't stay with it. The pull of their clarity is too strong, and their contaminated thinking is not powerful enough to keep them from it.

The average three-year-old:

- Tends to be deeply engaged, easily amused and satisfied with the simple joys of life; is present and in the moment, finding lots of things fun and funny.

- Is loving and open-hearted, connecting easily with others.

- Knows they don't really understand how life works; is curious, often puzzled, and constantly learning, coming up with new ideas and creative insights.

- Gets over upsets quickly and easily; doesn't tend to dwell on past mistakes or worry about the future.

- Is in touch with their deeper wisdom, often aware of "the elusive obvious" that the adults around them aren't seeing.

The average three-year-old spends a lot of their time in clarity, because they're allowing their psychology to do what it's designed to do. The psychology of little children is an example of the mind's self-correcting system given the freedom to do what it does best; return to a set point of clarity and well-being.

Your mind is a self-correcting system. Its set point is clarity, resilience and well-being... The benefits of allowing the mind to find its own way back to clarity vastly outweigh the benefits of external intervention.

Why? Because external intervention stops the self-correcting system doing its job.

Clarity is what a person's psychology is always endeavouring to return to. Innate clarity and resilience are always shining a beacon, even when a person seems hopelessly lost. You see...

Clarity isn't an achievement; it's a pre-existing condition...

It's not something you need to practice or "work on". It's an expression of who you really are.

The infinite creative intelligence of MIND shows up in every aspect of our experience, gently pointing us towards clarity and well-being. The capacity for clarity is there within each one of us, tirelessly working to guide us in the direction of our most inspiring, rewarding and meaningfully successful lives.

CLARITY equals **Capacity** minus **Contamination**

When you turn your attention away from the grinding familiarity of contaminated thinking, you make space for clarity, and the powerful inevitability of fresh, new thought. That's when you find yourself looking in the most generative, nourishing and resourceful direction there is…

keep exploring ⁖ connect with others
share your discoveries ⁖ deepen your understanding

Thought experiment: *What happens when you open to the possibility that clarity and peace of mind are your "default settings"?*

www.LittleBookOfClarity.com/chapter9

10

Creativity and Disruptive Innovation

....

"You don't learn to walk by following rules. You learn by doing, and by falling over."

Richard Branson, Entrepreneur, founder of Virgin Group

"It just occurred to me when I was out for a walk in the woods…"

In 2003, I started a business creating educational products. Each week, I wrote an article and sent it to my subscribers. By the end of the first year, 5000 people had subscribed to my articles, when I had a sudden insight. Google had recently launched "Adwords", the little adverts that show up when you search the web. I could run ads for my newsletter and pay a low price for each new subscriber. It was years before anyone else caught on.

By 2008, I had one of the largest email lists in the industry, with over 80,000 subscribers in my "tribe". I explained my adword "secret" to a marketing expert who was interviewing me, and he asked me where I got the idea. "I don't know," I said, "It just occurred to me when I was out for a walk in the woods."

Now I know where that innovative new idea came from; it came from the unknown...

DISTINCTION: The known vs. The unknown

- **The known** is the database of thoughts you've already thought, including your habitual ways of thinking about yourself, your life and your world.

- **The unknown** is the source of all fresh, new thoughts; the formless power of THOUGHT. When we have clarity, our minds are free from contaminated thinking, and we create space for new thinking to flow in.

Looking to the database of the known for navigating the future is like looking in the rear-view mirror to find your way forward...

When people are looking for solutions, they tend to look to what they already know, but all too often the answers we need can't be found there. When we want fresh new ideas, creativity, solutions and changes, it pays to look to the unknown.

Disruptive innovation

The music industry was like a rabbit in the headlights in 1999 when Napster enabled millions of users to share their music collections with each other. The record companies responded by clinging to a model designed for a world that no longer existed. They looked to the known for the answer, and came up empty-handed; their revenues dropped by 50% between 2001 and 2010. Meanwhile, Apple launched the iTunes store in 2003, making it possible for customers to purchase and download music online legally. Apple threw a life preserver to the music business, and gave their customers what they really wanted, becoming the world's most profitable company in the process.

The gap

Epistemologist Gregory Bateson said that problems result from the difference between how nature works and the way people think. If we try to navigate using an out-of-date map, we run into problems; our thinking is out of step with how the world is working. But the music industry (and many other businesses) clung to the map of their habitual thinking in the face of overwhelming evidence that it was no longer fit for purpose. Why?

Lack of clarity.

The only explanation for this bizarre behaviour is that they were lost in contaminated thinking, hypnotized by the outside-in mis-understanding, unable to see clearly. Contaminated thinking can make it seem as though the unknown is dangerous, and the database of habitual thinking is a safe refuge, but nothing could be further from the truth.

So what's the alternative? Insightful understanding. Insightful understanding closes the gap between how life works and how you *think* it works...

When do you get your best ideas?

Senior executives in the USA were surveyed and asked where and when they tended to get their best ideas. The top three answers were as follows:

1 On vacation

2 In the shower

3 While travelling to and from the office

Almost everyone can relate to this and find their own examples of fresh, new thought arriving when the mind is in a more relaxed, contemplative state. Yet, all too often, when people want to find an answer, solution or fresh new idea, they grind away at what they already know; running through their habitual thinking patterns one more time.

Throughout history, many of the most groundbreaking ideas came from the unknown, in the form of insights and sudden "a-ha" moments: Archimedes had his "eureka moment" as he climbed into his bath, and suddenly realized how to determine the volume of an object. Isaac Newton had his insight into the nature of gravity as he lay under an apple tree in his mother's garden. We all have a source of fresh new thinking, beyond what we already know...

- The insight that gives you the elegant solution for something which had you stumped.

- The realization that has you understand something which used to baffle you.

- The "a-ha moment" that gives you a fresh new perspective on a situation.

- The clear mind that allows you to remember where you left something you'd been frantically searching for.

Whether you call it an insight, a realization, or an "a-ha" moment, new arrivals from the unknown almost always come with a feeling of peace and clarity, a gentle rightness and "knowing" that feels fresh and new.

The known of our thinking is often like an out-of-date map that doesn't show any recent developments; the new streets, parks and paths of possibility. We can search the map as much as we like, but we won't find something wonderful that's just around the corner (or right there in front of us) if the map doesn't mention it.

So, if it's off the map, where can you find it? And how can you benefit from the clarity, resilience and peace of mind that it brings?

---

keep exploring ⁙ connect with others
share your discoveries ⁙ deepen your understanding

Thought experiment: *Just like there's no way to "un-stale" a loaf of bread, there's no way to freshen thinking that's past its use-by date. Fortunately, the principles behind clarity are like the baker's oven. They're always ready to produce fresh, new thinking as soon as it occurs to you that you won't find the answer in what you've already thought.*

www.LittleBookOfClarity.com/chapter10

11

Authenticity: Your True Identity

....

"Matter flows from place to place and momentarily comes together to be you. Whatever you are, therefore, you are not the stuff of which you are made."

Richard Dawkins, Evolutionary biologist

"You are not your job. You are not how much money you have in the bank…"

These two "un-firmations" echo through the 1999 film *Fight Club* like an incantation. And, while the film continues to detail "who you aren't" (you are not the shoes that you wear, the contents of your wallet, etc.), it's less specific about who you are…

A case of mistaken identity

Stop for a moment and touch your nose. Say the words "This is my nose."

I've invited countless members of my audiences, training groups and corporate teambuilding sessions to perform this simple task over the years. Everyone finds it easy to do, yet few of us consider the extraordinary accomplishments that make this possible.

When you were born, you didn't realize that you had a nose, eyes and a face. Your hands and fingers were mysterious objects that emitted sensations and occasionally bumped into your head. You had no sense of them being "yours", or of your being able to control them.

But then something amazing happened...

You started to make a map; a map of you. It started with your body, your immediate environment and your parents. This map let you define the relationships between different parts of your body – essential for being able to perform actions like touching your nose or grasping an object.

You also created a map of "who you are"; a map which you've been updating ever since. This map of "who you are" is sometimes called the self-image, self-concept or ego.

The self-image gets used as a reference point for living, giving you an opinion on what you're capable of, where your limits are, what you deserve, what's important, etc. Whether you think something's possible for you or not, it's likely that you automatically check with your self-image to find out its opinion, one way or another.

> But here's the thing: your self-image is just a THOUGHT-generated map/model. It's not who you really are.
>
> And while none of us would ever make the mistake of confusing a map of New York City with the city itself, we all make this same mistake when we confuse our self-image with who we really are.
>
> You see, just as a map of New York is not New York, your ideas about you are not you. We each fall into the trap of thinking our ideas about ourselves describe the entirety of who we are, but it's a case of mistaken identity.
>
> You are not your ideas about yourself.
>
> You are not the contents or structure of your thinking. And who you *really* are is far, far more than you think you are…

Who you *really* are is what's *creating* your experience; the intelligent, formless energy behind life; the principles behind clarity: THOUGHT, CONSCIOUSNESS and MIND.

It's odd to think of who we really are as "energy", but it also stands to reason. Science tells us that everything is made of energy, that the atoms that make up our bodies are mostly space.

Richard Dawkins suggests that we are more like waves than things. He explains that all the atoms that were in our bodies as children have been replaced; that whatever we may be, we're not the "stuff" of our physical bodies. Different cultures and traditions through the ages have had a variety of ways of describing what we are and where we come from:

- consciousness, soul, essence
- big mind, the great spirit, God
- natural intelligence, divine energy, the oneness

Each of these terms are metaphors pointing to a formless dimension.

Spiritual capacity and performance

In their January 2001 Harvard Business Review article, "The Making of a corporate Athlete", Jim Loehr and Tony Schwartz explain that, in addition to their physical, mental and emotional capacity, the most successful senior executives and entrepreneurs also attend to their "spiritual capacity", which they define as follows:

"By spiritual capacity, we simply mean the energy that is unleashed by tapping into one's deepest values and defining a strong sense of purpose.

This capacity, we have found, serves as sustenance in the face of adversity and as a powerful source of motivation, focus, determination, and resilience."

As you'll appreciate, the terms "deepest values" and "sense of purpose" are simply metaphors; forms that point to something deeper. Words like "team spirit" and "inspiration" are other examples of an attempt to point to something that comes *before* our world of form.

So how is this relevant?

Who you *really* are – your essence – is the formless energy behind life; the principles behind clarity. The principles of THOUGHT, CONSCIOUSNESS and MIND are also the source of your security, well-being, peace, joy and happiness, which means…

You already are what you've been searching for until now…

There's nothing to search for – you've already got it; you already *are* it. There's nowhere to get to – you're already here…

You don't need improving, fixing or developing – who you already *are* is the all-encompassing energy behind life!

So, if who we really are is this extraordinary intelligence – the formless energy behind life – why do we so often look, feel and act as though we're neither intelligent nor extraordinary? You guessed it: contaminated thinking, and the outside-in misunderstanding that gives rise to it.

It's entirely natural and understandable that we get fooled by our thinking. But we can each wake up to a greater clarity of understanding in any moment. No matter how deeply asleep we are, we're only ever one thought away from waking up. No matter how lost you sometimes get in dreams of lack, worry and insecurity, who you really are is always the same…

Peace, freedom, wisdom, clarity and love. You are what you've been searching for. Resilience, creativity, security, confidence and joy. You already are the source of all you desire: the energy behind life.

And just as a wave is not separate from the ocean, who you really are is not separate from the energy of the universe…

So how can you align yourself with how the world already works? Fortunately, you've been provided with an elegant, accurate and reliable tool for navigating life, deepening your understanding, guiding you back to clarity and having a richer experience than you may have ever thought possible…

keep exploring ⁘ connect with others
share your discoveries ⁘ deepen your understanding

Thought experiment: *What happens when you consider the fact that clarity, peace and security are only ever one thought away?*

www.LittleBookOfClarity.com/chapter11

12

Intuition: Navigating by Wisdom

....

"Don't let the noise of others' opinions drown out your own inner voice."

Steve Jobs, Entrepreneur, co-founder of Apple

(Stanford Commencement Speech, 2005[1])

"All that the pathfinder needs is his senses and knowledge of how to interpret nature's signs…"

In his book *Nature Is Your Guide: How to Find Your Way on Land and Sea*, record-breaking navigator Harold Gatty claims

---

[1] 'You've got to find what you love, Jobs says', Stanford Report, 14 June 2005 http://news.stanford.edu/news/2005/june15/jobs-061505.html

that there is no such thing as a sense of direction. He explains that a person who appears to have such a "sense" is actually using their five ordinary senses (seeing, hearing, smelling, tasting and feeling), informing and informed by their experience and intelligence.

Today we have GPS satellite navigation and numerous other technologies, yet we still rely on our senses for much of our day-to-day orientation. Whether we're walking down a city street, moving around our living space or driving to a friend's house, we're supported in our journeys by our five senses, our intelligence and our experience.

But we make a mistake when we try to use exactly the same "navigation system" to make our way through life. Consider these statements:

- "I want to get clarity on my overall life path before I take the next step."
- "I'm stuck. My life's at a roadblock and I need to get moving."
- "I need to define my values and purpose so I can start heading in the right direction."

Remember: people tend to think, speak and act as though their thought forms have the same qualities as the material world.

We use material-world *metaphors* for our work, then respond to them as though they're a material *reality.* We say that life's a journey, a struggle, or an adventure, then start behaving as though that's actually the case!

> *Fortunately, you have a* built-in *guidance system; it's called wisdom…*

It's a context-sensitive, up-to-the-minute, and comes from *before* your habitual thinking, from the intelligent energy behind life.

Sat-nav for your life

Even a map you made as recently as last week can't possibly respond to road closures and traffic jams, but a high-quality sat-nav can.

And where is the sat-nav of your wisdom navigating you to? It's helping you find your way back home to who you really are, so you can have a richer, deeper, more fulfilling experience of life… so you can enjoy the high performance and good decisions that come from a clear mind… so you can create what you're inspired to create… so you can benefit from the innovation, resilience and clarity you need to prosper in times of uncertainty, complexity and change.

You can think of this innate wisdom as an "emanation" from the formless energy behind life. Everybody has the wisdom of the universe within them. No one has access to more wisdom than anyone else. So, how do you become more and more open to wisdom, and allow it to guide you? It's *already* guiding you, moment to moment…

- When you're feeling more and more agitated as you think about something someone did last week... that's wisdom, activating the "psychological pain-withdrawal reflex".

- When you're lost in contaminated thinking, and it suddenly occurs to you that you're feeling your thinking... that's wisdom, pointing you back in the right direction.

- When you finally stop ruminating on a problem and the answer suddenly arrives... that's wisdom, penetrating the veneer of habitual thinking.

- When you're soaking in the tub and a flash of insight lets you know exactly how to proceed in an area where you were blocked... that's wisdom, giving you strategic guidance.

The wisdom that comes with clarity is typically accompanied by a good feeling; a sense of peaceful knowing that's very distinct from the "fervent rightness" of our habitual thinking.

Bear in mind that wisdom is looking out for your best interests. And while that doesn't mean that everyone's going to like what you do when you act on your wisdom, they'll often be able to "see the wisdom" in it. Wisdom often seems obvious in retrospect; people say things like "I don't understand how I didn't see it before." It's also worth remembering that wisdom is the source of insight, and that you've already been acting on it in a variety of ways throughout your life. It's good to see wisdom as the ordinary, everyday thing that it is. As you become more and more attuned to your wisdom, you may be surprised at just how easily you notice and are guided by it.

Strategic intuition

William Duggan is a senior lecturer in business management on Columbia University's MBA courses. In his award-winning book, *Strategic Intuition*, he explains that the flashes of insight that are so often the source of brilliant strategy almost never happen when people are thinking about the matter at hand.

Instead, they come when we're in the shower, or driving, or on holiday; when we're in a more reflective state, allowing our minds to wander.

As you allow yourself to be guided by wisdom, you create space for a deeper pattern of life to emerge. As you start living from a deeper understanding of the principles behind clarity, the circumstances of your life move into alignment with your deeper understanding.

So, does that mean that the circumstances of your life are all going to be a bed of roses? Not necessarily. Everyone has hardships to go through and losses to deal with. Furthermore, you don't know if your idea of what a great life looks like today will even *appeal* to you as you live life with a greater clarity of understanding.

So, if we're being guided by wisdom, where does that leave the whole domain of goal-setting?

I've got some good news and some bad news for you...

keep exploring ⁘ connect with others
share your discoveries ⁘ deepen your understanding

Thought experiment: *How good does it feel to realize that you have an incredibly reliable inner guidance system? A means of navigation that's always helping you out with clear, context-sensitive, up-to-the-minute information…*

www.LittleBookOfClarity.com/chapter12

13

Toxic Goals and Authentic Desires

....

"All great things are done for their own sake."

Robert Frost, Poet, playwright

"Escape 9–5, live anywhere, and join the new rich…"

I'd been working hard for five years, growing my business when I read Tim Ferriss' lifestyle-hacking manifesto, *The 4-Hour Work Week* in 2007. While I loved the products and services we offered, there was something missing, and I was convinced that Ferriss had put his finger on what it was; I needed to restructure the business so I could spend less time working and more time having adventures!

I met with my team, and we spent months analysing, streamlining and automating. By February 2008, I was ready to take my first "mini-retirement"; a three-month holiday to one of the world's premier ski-resorts.

"This is it!" I thought as I booked my tickets. "Finally, I'm going to have what I've been looking for. I'm going to be fulfilled, peaceful and exhilarated. I'm going to take my skiing to a new level, feel super-successful and have brilliant bragging rights."

But that's not how it worked out.

After the euphoria of the first week or two on the slopes had passed, I started feeling distracted, uneasy and bored, with a busy mind and sore feet. I was supposed to be on top of the world. Instead, I was in the doldrums! I had the *circumstances* of success, but I wasn't having the *experience* of success.

I flew home six weeks early and went back to the drawing board.

DISTINCTION: Toxic goals vs. Authentic desires

- **Toxic goals:** Toxic goals diminish a person's quality of life from the moment they set them. They reinforce the outside-in misunderstanding and encourage people to exchange a rich experience of the present moment for contaminated thinking; an idealized future concept.

• **Authentic desires:** Authentic desires are an expression of your innate clarity, wisdom and well-being. They're part of following your curiosity and fascination; things you want for their own sake. As a result, there's no sense of angst or lack with authentic desires; no sense of striving or "I'll be happy when…" When it's an authentic desire, you know you'll be fine whether you achieve it or not.

So am I saying you shouldn't have goals?

No, I'm not. Goals can be really useful tools for focusing your attention, marshalling your resources and measuring progress. But, just like any other tool, improper use can lead to injury. Toxic goals often take one of the following forms (you'll recognize some of these as having the "hidden hamster wheel" structure):

• I want [*goal*] so I can be [*happy / peaceful / secure / successful*].

• I want [*goal*] so I can stop feeling [*unhappy / insecure / not-ok*].

• I want [*goal*] because [*I think I should want it / I don't know what I really want / I'm afraid to go for what I really want*].

All these goal structures are based on the mistaken belief that our feelings come from something *other than* THOUGHT taking form in the moment. People typically respond to toxic goals in one of two ways. They either:

a struggle and strive, failing to achieve the toxic goal (sometimes for years), and finally give up with a sense of frustration and hopelessness, or…

b succeed in achieving the toxic goal, experience an initial rush of euphoria, then feel a sense of emptiness and lack. This is often accompanied by the sentiment "So that wasn't it either…", followed by the setting of yet another toxic goal (often "bigger and better" than the last one).

The two million pound security blanket

A few years ago, I was working with a client who had set himself a goal to raise 2.1 million pounds. He explained that he'd calculated 2.1 million pounds as the amount of money he needed to have in his bank account before he could feel a sense of security. Toxic goal alert! It raises an important question:

How secure can a person ever feel when they're believing that their security comes from something outside of them; something other than the principle of THOUGHT taking form in the moment?

Many toddlers have a security blanket or teddy bear. Psychologists refer to this as a "transitional object"; something that "gives" the child a sense of comfort and security in times of change or uncertainty (e.g. bedtime). Of course, we know that the blanket or teddy bear can't actually "give" the child a feeling of security or comfort; that can only come from within the child themselves. It just *seems* to the child as though the feelings come from the transitional object. But it doesn't work that way. It only works one way; inside-out.

Every adult knows that the child's security blanket involves a trick of the mind, but how often do we look to adult "teddy bears" (e.g., jobs, possessions, money, relationships) as though they're somehow different?

There's nothing wrong with material success. But you're much more likely to enjoy it when you build it on your sense of *inner* security and *true* peace of mind.

Toxic goals are contaminated thoughts. You weren't born thinking them, and you were motivated to learn to walk and to talk. You were motivated to use your hands, to play and to explore. You were motivated to make and create; to love and connect with other people. And you still are, whether you're already aware of it or not.

So how can we relate to goals in a way that is fulfilling, productive and healthy?

Case Study: Authentic desire, vision and direction

Joe Stumpf had spent 20 years building an incredibly successful business, "By Referral only", providing support to real estate agents and mortgage brokers in the USA. Every month, for the previous two decades, he'd flown to a different town or city to run a boot camp to help agents and brokers start getting their businesses on track. Not only were these events the first step in Joe's sales and marketing funnel, but Joe also saw himself as a torch-bearer, bringing knowledge and hope to people who, when they first met him, were often struggling to make a living. His business specialized in helping them move out of struggle and into stability and success (many of Joe's formerly struggling clients go on to serve as de facto mentors to others). Joe asked me to coach him because he was at a point of transition and was feeling stuck. He was proud of the business he'd created, but he no longer wished to fly from city to city each month. He knew that phase of his business was finished, but didn't know what the next phase was. He wanted a new vision for his business and himself, so I worked with Joe to help him find clarity. He emerged with an inspiring vision for his business, and for his role in it. Joe says: "The insights I gleaned from our session resulted in one of the most important directional shifts of my life." Joe's business has shifted to not just being a training company, but to also being an information publisher and service provider. It's continued to go from strength to strength, despite the economic downturn. And, just as importantly, Joe's following his heart and living life on his own terms. He recently took on the challenge of being the oldest man ever to survive the civilian version of the navy seal "Hell Week" (at age 54), and he's just written a book called *Willing Warrior*.

One of the great things about authentic desires is that they don't need to be realistic; you want what you want, whether you think it's possible for you or not. When you discover an authentic desire, you may have no idea how you're going to achieve it. That's OK. When you step into the unknown, and keep moving forward, your wisdom will guide you in discovering the path (the "how"). If you're willing to "make a space" for your authentic desires, and take action, you'll be amazed at where they will lead you.

Reality check

"What about targets, goals and objectives set by other people – my boss, for instance? He sets me toxic goals all the time, but I don't have the luxury of replacing them with authentic desires."

Another person can set you a goal that you don't *like*, but the only thing that can make it "toxic" is your own contaminated thinking; the idea that your happiness, security of peace of mind is in some way bound up in it. You may say *"But I have to do it or I'll lose my job – it's like having a gun to my head."*

The idea that your happiness, security or well-being are dependent on your keeping your job is a great example of the outside-in misunderstanding. Looking to a job for security is like looking to a toaster for peace of mind; it's not that jobs and toasters aren't useful – they just can't give you what you can only find inside of you. One of the things you'll begin to notice as you continue deepening your understanding of the principles behind clarity is that tasks which used to bother you become less and less of an issue. If you're willing to "make a space" for your authentic desires, and take action, you'll be amazed at where they will lead you.

Once you realize that your clarity, security and well-being isn't dependent on setting or achieving goals, then you can relax, and allow your wisdom to guide you. As you begin to realize you don't need anything to be OK, you also realize there's no urgent need to uncover your authentic desires; they'll emerge in their own time.

In the meantime, stay in the game. 80% of success is showing up, and authentic desires often find you when and where you least expect it.

So, with that in mind, I'd like to take you somewhere very special, to a place that holds the answers to all your questions, and the solutions to all your problems…

---

keep exploring ⁘ connect with others
share your discoveries ⁘ deepen your understanding

Thought experiment: *As you're reading this now, are there any "toxic goals" that still look like a reality to you? In contrast, what are some of the authentic desires that you're already starting to become aware of?*

www.LittleBookOfClarity.com/chapter13

14

The Power of Presence

"We convince by our presence."

Walt Whitman, Poet and journalist

"It's… Uhh… Ahh… Umm…"

The location was St Lucia, and it was the third day of one of my *Life Transformation Retreats*. One of the participants had just had a profound insight (signalled with a loud "OH!" and a look of sudden realization). Everyone in the group turned to him, eager to hear about the pearl of wisdom that had just been revealed to him. He opened his mouth to speak, and said *"It's… uhh… ahh… umm…"*. He stopped, furrowed his brow, then tried again. This time, no sounds came out; his mouth just opened and closed as the expression on his face cycled through a variety of emotions: surprise, confusion, puzzlement, amusement, peace…

His habitual thinking had been massively interrupted; he'd woken up to the present moment.

Being present

Being present is often described as having your attention on what's happening in the present moment. But there's more to it (and less to it) than that…

> *"Present" is whatever is happening moment to moment, prior to your habitual thinking.*

So, how does our habitual thinking take us out of the present moment? By creating THOUGHT-objects that take us into the future or the past. These THOUGHT-objects can take a variety of forms, for example:

• Toxic goals	• Remembering	• Fear of loss
• Worrying	• Ruminating	• Comparing
• Anxiety	• Judgements	• Validation-seeking
• Daydreaming	• Imagining	• Attention-seeking
• Resentments	• Planning	• etc.

But here's the thing:

There is only ever this moment. The present is all there is... The future and the past are THOUGHT-generated illusions... Illusions that you only ever experience in the here and now...

Thought Experiment

Try this out: remember an enjoyable experience from the past. One hundred per cent of your experience of that memory is taking place in the present moment; none of it is happening in the past. Now imagine something you're going to do in the future. 100% of your experience of that imagined event is taking place in the present moment; none of it is happening in the future. When you find yourself in the "now", it's an indication that you're not caught up in your habitual thinking.

As you continue exploring the principles behind clarity, you'll start finding your way into a state of meditation, free from contaminated thinking, more and more frequently. So does this mean you'll find yourself cross-legged, chanting "Ommm" in the middle of business meetings? Fortunately not.

Just as insights are "context sensitive", so is clarity. The meditative states you find yourself enjoying will be "fit for purpose" bringing you what you need, when you need it.

The athlete's clarity (aka "the zone") when they're performing at their best has a different flavour to the computer programmer's clarity (aka "flow"). While they're both expressions of clarity, they're configured to meet different requirements. They're different again from the tranquil, meditative state that arises when you're getting away from it all, looking at the sunset, the ocean or little fluffy clouds. But all have three things in common: clarity of mind, access to the resources you need and being present to the moment.

Your deepening understanding of the principles behind clarity will bring you more and more fully into the present, with everything you need to respond effectively in the moment.

When you're out of our habitual thinking, you're more closely aligned with reality. When you're in the present, you're responsive to what's happening, with the clarity that comes from being more deeply connected with life.

Clear mind, more time

One of the things I often hear from my clients when they start exploring the principles behind clarity is how much extra time they have. Whenever a client says this, I make a point of asking what they attribute this extra time to. Their answer usually includes one or more of the points on this list:

- The amount of time they're no longer wasting in insecure, outside-in thinking such as worry and anxiety

- More intuitive decision-making, with less time wasted stressing and more time spent in "flow".

- More elegant, leveraged ways of getting things done and achieving results.

- Better ideas and creative solutions to problems.

- Better performance, resulting in greater impact, fewer errors and less re-work.

- A richer experience of the present moment; getting more "juice" from their day.

> *The outside-in misunderstanding is the biggest time thief there is. If it wasn't for our contaminated thinking, we'd discover that every day brings a 1:1 match of time and enterprise. When we're present, with a clear mind, we have what we need for the task at hand. We intuitively know when to pause and when to press on; when to rest and when to proceed...*

CLARITY equals **Capacity** minus **Contamination**

This doesn't necessarily mean that on a daily basis you're going to work out at the gym, answer all your email, and clear your to-do list. Your habitual thoughts about what you believe you *should* be doing is not necessarily part of this 1:1 match of time and enterprise. But as you continue to explore the principles behind clarity, you'll discover the implicit connection between presence, performance and perfect timing.

When you fall out of your habitual thinking and into the present, you slip out of the outside-in misunderstanding about how life works. The idea that your well-being is being held hostage by a given problem or issue often drops away, and clarity emerges. Strange as it may seem, you discover that all is well in this moment.

Reality Check

You may be saying "What about problems that need solving urgently? If I lose my job, clarity isn't going to help me pay the bills!" Life has its ups and downs. While some hardships are inevitable for each of us, there are two things that mean we can deal with any situation we encounter:

1 We each have within us a source of security, well-being and resilience.

2 We each have within us a source of clarity, wisdom and guidance.

In fact, these things aren't just *within* you; they *are* you. Clarity, wisdom and resilience are your *nature*. The knowledge that clarity comes from within, combined with your innate guidance system gives you everything you need to deal with the ups and downs of life.

All over the world, on a daily basis, people lose jobs, get divorced, lose loved ones and get injured. We all get dealt our share of hurts, hardships and disappointments. People's responses to these misfortunes range from denial, trauma and shutdown, to reflection, acceptance and bounce-back. When you have clarity, you realize you have what you need to respond appropriately and deal with what comes your way.

You see, there's something utterly reliable that everyone's got, but that very few people *realize* they have. Something that means you don't have to worry; that you've got what it takes to handle what comes your way...

***keep exploring ⁖ connect with others
share your discoveries ⁖ deepen your understanding***

Thought experiment: *"If it wasn't for our contaminated thinking, we'd discover that every day brings a 1:1 match of time and enterprise." Consider this curious statement. Then reflect on the fact that, if it wasn't for contaminated thinking, you'd find every activity you undertake to be engaging, absorbing and fulfilling.*

www.LittleBookOfClarity.com/chapter14

15

Resilience

....

"Our greatest glory is not in never falling, but in rising every time we fall."

Confucius, Philosopher

"There's no place like home... there's no place like home..."

In the film *The Wizard of Oz*, the heroine (Dorothy, played by Judy Garland) gets caught in a tornado, and wakes up in the strange land of Oz. She's desperate to find her way home to Kansas, and goes on a quest to meet the wizard who she believes holds the key to her return.

At the end of the story, Dorothy discovers that she has the power she needs within her. She taps her ruby slippers together, repeats the phrase "There's no place like home" and wakes up in her bed, surrounded by her family. Dorothy doesn't believe them when they first tell her the adventure in Oz was a nightmare. She protests that it was a real place, but they reassure her that she never left her home; that it was just a dream…

We've all had the experience of waking up from a dream so realistic that we thought it had actually happened; felt the sense of gratitude and relief as the racing pulse of nightmare gives way to the reality of the here and now. The dream reality seems so real that we mistake it for a material reality. But all along, the dreamer is tucked up in bed, sleeping soundly, perfectly safe.

Our clarity and peace of mind have a natural buoyancy. Like a football being held underwater, as soon as you let go, it rises to the surface. It doesn't matter how long you've been holding it there, or how much effort you've put into it; the moment you let go, its natural buoyancy begins to lift it. And, just as a football's natural buoyancy is an implication of the principle of gravity, your clarity and resilience are implications of the principles of MIND, THOUGHT and CONSCIOUSNESS.

When we're lost in contaminated thinking, we sometimes experience feelings of worry, agitation, urgency, etc. Due to a trick of the mind, we tend to "blame" those low feelings on something *other than* the principle of THOUGHT taking form in the moment. The moment we do that, we also give our power away, and feel we urgently need to solve our problems, achieve our goals, and make changes in our lives.

The worse we feel, the more urgent and compelling those external changes can seem.

But, as clarity emerges, we wake up into a deeper, more connected experience of life. Suddenly the things we'd been perceiving as problems look different; they disappear, we see obvious solutions, or just feel confident that we'll find a way forward. Our creativity comes to the surface, and our natural resourcefulness and resilience come into play. We intuitively know that we'll be OK no matter what, and that we can trust our wisdom to guide us.

Reality Check

Am I suggesting that you stick your head in the sand and ignore your problems? No! But I *am* suggesting that your ability to perceive something as a problem in the *first place* is an expression of your habitual thinking and level of understanding. As you see the situation more clearly, everything looks different, including what you'd been perceiving as a problem.

We've all experienced this. We struggle with an issue for hours, days or even longer, then one morning we wake up and either a) We no longer see it as a problem or b) We see a solution that seems so obvious, we can't believe we didn't think of it sooner. You are innately resilient; clarity and peace of mind are always there, just a thought away.

Of course, we all have an innate understanding of the inside-out nature of life at the core of our consciousness; it's what we're "made of" at the most essential level. So, as you keep looking in this direction, and allowing insight to dissolve the outside-in misunderstanding, it's inevitable that your increasing clarity of understanding will continue rising. And the higher it rises, the more clarity of thought you'll find yourself experiencing.

Life is not a problem to be solved

The philosopher Kierkegaard wisely said that life is not a problem to be solved; that it's a mystery to be experienced. When we lose our clarity of thought, we innocently look at life as a series of problems to be solved and goals to be achieved. But the agitation and urgency are actually our wisdom signals...

- reminding us that we're living in the feeling of THOUGHT taking form...

- pointing us in the direction of clarity, possibility and peace of mind...

- guiding us to look away from the *content* of our experience, and towards that which is *creating* our moment to moment experience; the formless principles of MIND, THOUGHT and CONSCIOUSNESS.

As you start to see how these principles are playing out in your life (and always have been), you can start living more and more in clarity, insight and a deeper felt experience of life. You'll still have your ups and downs but, behind them, is the knowledge of your inner resilience and the default-setting of your innate clarity and well-being.

Near the end of The Wizard of Oz, Glinda the good witch reveals that Dorothy has *always* had the power to get home, but that she wouldn't have believed it if she'd been told at the beginning; she had to discover it for herself. When asked what she's learned, Dorothy says *"If I ever go looking for my heart's desire again, I won't look any further than my own backyard. Because if it isn't there, I never really lost it to begin with!"*

You'll find that your habitual contaminated thinking tends to be about "me and my circumstances" (How am I doing? What do I need? How do I look to others? What if I lose this? How can I get that? I'll be happy when… / I can't be happy because… etc.). It looks real, so you get fooled into searching and seeking outside yourself for something that's already there within you. When we get caught up in contaminated thinking, we innocently mistake it for a material reality. But it's not a reality – it's just a dream.

The dream-reality seems so real that we mistake it for a material reality. But, all along, the dreamer is tucked up in bed, sleeping soundly, perfectly safe. Everyone has dreams of isolation and insecurity from time to time but, in any moment, you can wake up to the reality of who you really are…

- you are the dreamer…
- you are the thinker…
- you are not the dream; you are what's *dreaming* the dream…
- you are not your thoughts; you are what's *creating* the thoughts…

123

You are not your experience;
you are what's generating your experience;
Mind, the power principle,
the "intelligent energy" behind life…

In any moment, you can wake up to the truth of who you
really are, and live life more fully from clarity, insight and
peace of mind…

So, if the dream of isolation is an illusion, what's the deeper reality behind life? If you are the dreamer, perfectly safe, what's the truth of the domain you're resting in? And what awaits you as you continue waking up?

---

keep exploring ⁘ connect with others
share your discoveries ⁘ deepen your understanding

Thought experiment: *Isn't it a relief to realize that clarity, security and peace of mind are always on hand? Ready to rise to the surface, no matter what, as soon as you insightfully realize that you're feeling the principle of Thought taking form in the moment?*

www.LittleBookOfClarity.com/chapter15

16

Connection and Relationships

....

"Despite our habit of seeing ourselves as separate, solid 'things,' our minds, our beings are not fixed. We exist in a web of relationships."

Joseph Jaworski, Author and Founder of The American Leadership Forum

"Make me one with everything…"

The punchline to the old joke about the Buddhist and the hotdog vendor casts a light on one of life's most persistent illusions. It certainly looks like we're separate from each other, and from the natural world. But, strange as it may seem, there's a way in which separation is an illusion. In reality, the fact that everything is made of energy means, in a very empirical sense, that we are all connected; with one another and with the rest of the universe.

We don't need anyone or anything to "make us" one with everything. We already *are* one with everything; we always have been and we always will be. However...

As we get caught up in contaminated thinking, we experience the *illusion* of separation from other people, and from life. The more contaminated thinking we're in, the more separate we feel.

And what does this have to do with connection and relationships?

> *The <u>true</u> source of loneliness, isolation and most conflict is the mistaken belief that we're feeling something other than the principle of* THOUGHT *taking form in the moment; that we're at the mercy of a world "out there" with power over how we feel.*

The *experience* of connection is incredibly valuable. In addition to the fact that it's natural and feels good, connection opens up a conduit for effective communication. When another person feels connected to you, they're much more likely to see where you're coming from, hear what you have to say and be impacted by what you're sharing with them.

> *Connection, intimacy and love are what's already there for us when there's nothing else in the way...*

So what gets in the way? Habitual patterns of contaminated thinking. But as your understanding of the principles behind clarity increases, contaminated thinking falls away and you start experiencing greater connection in all your relationships...

CLARITY equals **Capacity** minus **Contamination**

Listening to be impacted

A few years ago, I was at a meeting where one of the participants asked for help with an issue he'd been struggling with. He gave a brief outline of the problem (he'd been having trouble finding the right direction for his business) then the other participants started jumping in with solutions. I just listened. When the first round of solution-giving was over, I asked if it would be OK to do some exploring. He and the other participants agreed, so I asked him questions, then listened as deeply as I could to his answers. A feeling of connection started to develop, and he became reflective. All of a sudden, his face lit up. "I need to have more passion and adventure in what I'm doing", he said. Over the weeks and months that followed, he started making the necessary changes to move in a new direction.

When you listen deeply, and allow a connection to emerge, the resulting conversations can be profound, creative and extremely useful.

Two worlds in one

Imagine you're watching a film at the cinema. As you look at the characters on the screen, you experience them as separate people – figures moving against a background. Our ability to experience them as distinct from each other (and from the background) is what allows us to transform the patterns of light on the screen into individual characters. This in turn allows us to experience the drama of the film as it unfolds.

But the seemingly separate figures on the screen are actually part of an unbroken continuum of light and shadow. The distinctions between the characters, and between figure and ground, are mind-made illusions, generated from within us. The same goes for all the feelings we experience as we watch the movie.

The film is neutral; 100% of our experience of (and response to) the film arises from within us.

Now, let's go one step further. The flow of images on the screen is only there because light is shining from a projector at the back of the cinema. The patterns of light on the screen have no existence independent of the projector and the reel of film it's playing. Form and formless are one, a unified whole. Switch off the light and the movie disappears from the screen.

The tangible illusion of the film on the screen has no existence separate from the (relatively) intangible reality of the light shining from the projector.

It's the same with us. Our experience of the world of form (including each other) is a tangible illusion; tangible, but not real. The principles behind clarity represent a deeper reality; intangible, but real, giving rise to the tangible illusion of the material world.

> *Just as the images on the screen have no existence*
> *independent of the light from the projector...*
>
> *And just as a wave has no existence separate from*
> *the ocean...*
>
> *The material world of form in all its glory has no existence*
> *separate from the formless energy behind life...*
>
> *Form and formless are one, a unified whole...*

When you're asleep and dreaming, your experience of the characters, environments and situations is created from *within your consciousness.* It's the same when you're awake. Remember: 100% of your experience of the world "outside" of you is actually taking place inside of you, generated from deep within your consciousness (albeit with a live data feed via your senses). The principles behind clarity give rise to our experience of reality. Our personal thoughts, perceptions and self-images are like waves; we can notice them, obsess about them, even take ownership of them. But they have no existence separate from the whole. They don't "belong" to us any more than a droplet of water "belongs" to a given whirlpool or wave.

As our clarity of understanding increases, something amazing begins to happen. Life starts looking less complex, and we begin to see a simplicity behind many of the challenges people face. In fact, in a world that appears beset by a dizzying array of complex issues and seemingly impossible problems, there's a realization that can offer genuine hope and practical solutions...

---

keep exploring ⁓ connect with others
share your discoveries ⁓ deepen your understanding

Thought experiment: *"Connection, intimacy and love are what's already there for us when there's nothing else in the way."* What would it mean for you and your various relationships if this were true?

www.LittleBookOfClarity.com/chapter16

PART THREE

The Way Forward

17

There's Only One Problem

....

"When I am working on a problem, I never think about beauty but when I have finished, if the solution is not beautiful, I know it is wrong."

R. Buckminster Fuller, Designer and inventor

"Behind the London riots a multitude of causes..."

The Euronews headline from August 9, 2011 attempted to make sense of the riots that had started that week in London (sparked by the tragic shooting of Mark Duggan by police marksmen), then spread to other cities in the UK. The "causes" identified in the days that followed ranged from poor parenting and gang culture to budget cuts, social media and consumerism. But what if this dizzying array of societal, family and individual "causes" were actually not causes, but *effects*; the emergent properties of a single, underlying cause?

The lime solution

During the early 1800s, countless women were dying of puerperal fever, a bacterial infection contracted during childbirth. At the time, the illness was attributed to a mind-boggling variety of causes (ranging from bad smells and "atmospheres" to overcrowding, constipation, vigorous exercise, posture during labour and psychological factors).

In the 1840s, a Hungarian doctor, Ignaz Semmelweis, noticed that women who gave birth at home, in the midwives' ward or even in the street had a much lower incidence of puerperal fever than those who gave birth in the doctors' ward of his hospital. He had a sudden insight: the illness was being spread by something invisible on the hands and instruments of the doctors.

In May of 1847, Semmelweis ordered that all doctors in his hospital wash their hands in a chlorinated lime solution before contact with the patients. The rate of puerperal fever fell from 18% to less than 3%.

The theories of the day had identified dozens of "causes," but there was in fact just one cause: germs and bacteria on the unwashed hands and instruments of the doctors.

Sadly, the medical orthodoxy of the day thought Semmelweis' discovery was too simplistic, and lacked credibility. Semmelweis' practice of hand-washing didn't become widespread until many years later.

Is it credible that a single cause is responsible for the London riots, just as a single cause was responsible for puerperal fever? If so, what could possibly explain such a diverse and complex array of effects?

A misunderstanding: The misguided belief that we're feeling something *other than* the principle of THOUGHT taking form in the moment. This misunderstanding leads to contaminated thinking just as surely as the misunderstanding of germs and bacteria leads to contaminated surgical instruments.

- If a person believes their security, happiness and well-being comes from amassing money and wealth, then they're likely to become *greedy.*

- If a person believes their agitated feelings are caused by other people, then they're likely to experience *resentment, hostility* and other *relationship problems.*

- If a person's habitual thinking is standing between them and their deeper feelings of peace and well-being, then they're likely to be *unhappy.*

- If a person believes their security comes from money, and their money supply starts looking unstable, then *anxiety* and *neediness* are understandable responses.

- If a person doesn't realize that they have a source of wisdom within them, and makes important decisions when they're clouded with contaminated thinking, they're going to make some *bad decisions.*

- If a person doesn't realize that they are profoundly *resilient*, and they see trouble on the horizon, then they're likely to *worry*.

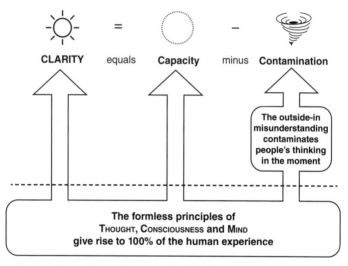

Figure 17.1   Contamination: The Outside-in Misunderstanding

It doesn't take a huge leap of creativity to trace most of the day's news topics to a small number of culprits: neediness, greed, anxiety, stress, anger, resentment and lack of wisdom. And all these culprits are symptoms of a single problem: contaminated thinking resulting from the outside-in misunderstanding.

The theories of the day had identified dozens of "causes",
but there was in fact just one cause…

Reality Check

You may be saying "What about things like natural disasters, unavoidable accidents, diseases and dementia? There are lots of problems that *aren't* down to contaminated thinking!"

True. Life has its ups and downs, and no one gets through it without their share of challenges. Seeing the inside-out nature of reality and living from a clearer, more profound felt experience of life won't stop that. But it gives us a) the resilience to know we can deal with whatever comes our way, and b) the wisdom, clarity and creativity to make a difference in our own lives and in the lives of others going forward.

It turns out that life is less about what happens to you, and more about how you relate to it…

In the past 100 years alone, insight and creativity has resulted in discoveries which have made a massive difference in the lives of millions. Alexander Fleming's discovery of penicillin in 1928 has resulted in the lives of countless people being saved.

But what if there were a kind of "penicillin for the mind" that could have as dramatic an effect on your clarity, your character and your behaviour as antibiotics have had on bacterial infection?

keep exploring ⁚⁚ connect with others
share your discoveries ⁚⁚ deepen your understanding

Thought experiment: *What happens when you consider the possibility that the vast majority of the problems faced by society, businesses and individuals are the result of a single cause? A misunderstanding of the nature of* THOUGHT?

www.LittleBookOfClarity.com/chapter17

18

Penicillin for the Mind

....

"No problem can be solved from the same level of consciousness that created it."

Albert Einstein, Physicist, winner of the Nobel Prize in Physics, 1921

"There's nothing in this world that you can't turn into heroin…"

During an unexpectedly moving scene in the comedy *Get Him to the Greek* (2010, Universal Pictures), drug-addicted rock star Aldous Snow (played by Russell Brand) tries to convince his ex-girlfriend (played by Rose Byrne) to get back together with him. She explains that she's drug-free, and that the past few months have been the happiest of her life. He protests that he was clean for seven years when they were together. She replies "And you did yoga for five hours a day. That's mental! There's nothing in this world that you can't turn into heroin."

"Symptom substitution" is widely accepted in the world of traditional addiction treatment. The smoker gives up cigarettes but starts eating chocolate. The reformed cocaine addict becomes a workaholic. The alcoholic stops drinking and starts compulsively attending meetings. The surface behaviour has changed, often to something less damaging, but the habitual thought patterns (and the consciousness behind them) remain the same. By the same token, we can all think of examples of people who have had a sudden insight: a change of heart that dramatically impacts their life…

- The alcoholic who experiences a "moment of clarity", stops drinking for good, and becomes a valuable member of their community.

- The smoker who suddenly decides that "enough is enough", and easily gives up a habit that they were previously enslaved by.

- The workaholic businessman who has a heart attack, massively re-evaluates his priorities, downsizes and starts working a four-hour day so he can spend more time with his family.

These changes of heart are often regarded as psychological anomalies, sometimes labelled as "spontaneous remission" and given no further attention. Yet they are examples of a natural quality that we all have: The capacity for an increase in our clarity of understanding; a rise in our level of consciousness.

A rise in consciousness means a <u>permanent</u> increase in your clarity of understanding...

The infinite elevator

Imagine a sturdy, see-through elevator running up the side of an infinitely tall skyscraper at the centre of a crowded metropolis. When you first step into the elevator all you can see is the cars at street level and the buildings that surround you.

As the elevator begins to move, you start rising above the smaller buildings, and your sight line becomes less cluttered. The cars appear to grow smaller and smaller, and you can see the rooftops of the neighbouring office blocks. Soon, all but the tallest buildings are disappearing beneath you, and you can see far into the distance.

You admire the gentle transition as the population becomes less dense; from high-rises, to low-rises, to suburbs to countryside. As you continue your upward journey, the details of the city streets shrink into invisibility, and your eye is drawn to the sweep of the horizon. Eventually you start to become aware of the curvature of the Earth.

Your consciousness is like this infinite elevator. A rise in consciousness means an increase in clarity of understanding that brings you peace, perspective and greater clarity of mind.

The principle of CONSCIOUSNESS brings your thinking to life. When you experience a rise in your consciousness, the habits of thinking you previously experienced as a reality suddenly start losing their power. As your consciousness continues rising, you become more and more able to see your THOUGHT-generated experiential realities for the illusions that they are.

A rise in consciousness means a permanent increase in your clarity of understanding...

Penicillin for the mind

A rise in consciousness is like a kind of "penicillin for the mind". Penicillin can help our bodies to heal infection by inhibiting the growth and spread of illness-causing bacteria. Similarly, a rise in consciousness can transform how we relate to (and can even eliminate) huge amounts of contaminated thinking. Just as penicillin acts wherever in the body it's needed, a rise in consciousness goes to wherever it's needed in a person's psyche. A person whose consciousness rises often experiences an "across the board" increase in well-being, with issues they'd been perceiving as problems suddenly reducing in intensity, or even disappearing...

Case Study: Fear of conflict and public speaking

Tiffany was afraid to express her point of view during meetings at work, particularly if there was negativity, or if she disagreed with the points others were making. She came to one of my programmes, and we chatted about the principles behind clarity. The following week she found herself able to speak freely during her team meeting, even though she knew other people disagreed with her. She even gave a presentation to the group (something she'd been avoiding doing for months due to a fear of public speaking). Tiffany told me afterwards that she found the presentation so straightforward that she couldn't understand why she'd ever thought it was a problem. She had an insight – a rise in her level of understanding – and her innate clarity, resilience and well-being took care of the rest. It acted where it was needed.

DISTINCTION: Achievement-obsession vs. Understanding-orientation

- **Achievement-obsession:** If a person believes we live in an outside-in world, it's logical for them to be achievement-obsessed; to focus tirelessly on achieving goals and eliminating problems.

- **Understanding-orientation:** Once a person has even an *inkling* that we live in an inside-out world, it makes sense to adopt an understanding-orientation; you recognize that your embodied understanding of how life works is your biggest leverage point in whatever you want to accomplish.

Here's a way of thinking about it. Imagine two doctors living in London in the 1850s. Doctor A believes that illness and disease are caused by bad smells. He spends every available hour on a scheme to supply highly-scented flowers to every hospital ward in the city. He's totally focused on this *achievement*, because he wants the best for his patients. Doctor B is looking in a different direction. He's heard suggestions that illness and disease aren't caused by bad smells, but rather by tiny invisible creatures called germs and bacteria. He spends his time exploring this new *understanding*, because he wants the best for his patients.

Paradoxically, when you start to shift to an understanding orientation, it often "raises the bar" on what you're able to achieve. I've seen this in my own life, and in the lives of my clients: many of your biggest achievements come *after* you let go of an achievement-obsession, and start increasing your clarity of understanding.

Paradoxically, the things people have been perceiving as "problems" diminish in intensity or disappear. Mountains get turned back into molehills, and people find that they have the resources to tackle the things that *do* need dealing with, guided by their innate wisdom.

Reality Check

Am I saying there's anything wrong with wanting to achieve things? No, I'm not! But there's a huge difference between achievement that's driven by the sense of need and lack (the "I'll be happy when" of contaminated thinking) and the achievement that comes as a natural expression of following your wisdom, secure in the knowledge that you are *already* enough.

The morphine of self-improvement

Outside my window stands a strong, healthy tree, about forty feet tall. Many years ago, a seed was planted in the ground, and it started growing. The roots reach down into the nourishing soil, creating a strong foundation; the leaves absorb sunlight and carbon dioxide, transforming them into life-giving nutrients; the branches and leaves drink in the falling rain. The tree continues growing.

The tree doesn't "work on" growing. It just grows. Growing is its nature.

There's a way in which our attempts to "take control" of our personal evolution can actually interfere with our natural propensity to grow. The seeker's habitual searching is the very thing that stands in the way of them finding what they yearn for. Like an opiate, the intoxicating patterns of struggle and striving numb their emotional pain, while blinding them to the natural joy of living.

"There's nothing in this world that you can't turn into heroin…"

But, like the tree in my garden, growing is your nature. Clarity of understanding unlocks the self-love, gratitude and acceptance that are the sunlight, rainwater and nutrients of your personal evolution. While you don't get to decide the timescale, increases in consciousness and clarity of understanding are *inevitable* for you when you get out of your own way, let wisdom guide you and start enjoying your life as it is today.

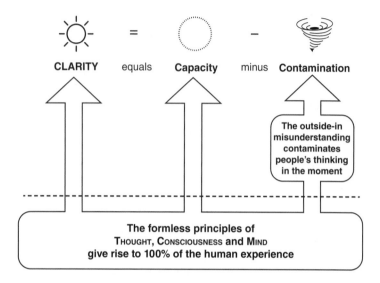

CLARITY equals Capacity minus Contamination

The outside-in misunderstanding contaminates people's thinking in the moment

The formless principles of THOUGHT, CONSCIOUSNESS and MIND give rise to 100% of the human experience

I realize that an understanding-orientation might seem like a counterintuitive choice for someone living in the "real world" of work, families, goals, businesses, mortgages, health and relationships. But as you follow your wisdom and keep increasing your understanding of the inside-out nature of life, you're going to be guided in living a life you love, no matter what.

So what do you need to do in order for that to happen?

keep exploring ⁘ connect with others
share your discoveries ⁘ deepen your understanding

Thought experiment: *What would happen if you decided not to treat yourself as a "thing" to be improved, and instead open to the possibility that it's your nature to continue learning, growing and evolving?*

There's an entire industry built on the assumption that it's a good idea to relate to yourself as a thing to be improved and worked on. Lots of people will be happy to tell you that makes sense. And while it's fine to take dancing lessons, or learn another language, you cross the line when you start pretending that your "self" needs improving. This one's worth reflecting on for a while.

www.LittleBookOfClarity.com/chapter18

19

Do Nothing

....

"The Master doesn't try to be powerful; thus he is truly powerful."

Lao Tse, Philosopher

"Point yourself in the right direction and do nothing..."

This provocative statement seemed to fly in the face of everything I "knew" about how to live an inspiring, successful life. Yet, while it was easy for the thrash-metal band of my habitual thinking to raise objections to this statement, I could also feel a truth in it. After all, I was a master of "doing"; I'd accomplished a lot in my life by taking action, but a lot of my "doing" had me running on the hamster wheel of "I'll be happy when..." thinking.

DISTINCTION: Misguided action vs. Inspired action

- **Misguided action** is action sponsored by the mistaken belief that it will lead to results which either give a person the felt experience they desire, or stop them from experiencing the feelings which they want to avoid. The contaminated thinking behind misguided action is often tinged with striving, urgency and desperation.

- **Inspired action** is action taken from the clarity of the inside-out understanding; the knowledge (at least intuitively) that your felt experience can't be threatened or delivered by anything other than the principle of THOUGHT taking form in the moment. Acting from this clarity is the essence of high-performance, what athletes, dancers and musicians sometimes refer to as being in flow.

When a person is acting from clarity, they'll still have powerful intuitions about the importance of timing, but there's rarely a feeling of stressful urgency. That's one of the reasons inspired action can be so effective and impactful.

So what does it mean to "Point yourself in the right direction and do nothing…"?

Pointing yourself in the right direction means looking towards what's creating your experience of life; looking to the *source* of your experience rather than the *content* of your experience.

And what's creating your experience of life? The principles behind clarity.

When we're caught up in contaminated thinking, we're fixated on the form of life. Our thinking always looks real, so it can seem as though we should be obsessing about the form our thinking is taking. When we're seeing how life really works (inside-out), we move back towards clarity, and are in a better position to be guided by wisdom.

In any moment, we can turn our gaze from the *content* of our experience (what we're thinking about) to what's *creating* our experience (the principles of THOUGHT, MIND and CONSCIOUSNESS.)

"Doing nothing" isn't about the actions you *take* so much as it is about the mindset that gives *rise* to your actions.

Most people spend much of their lives taking misguided action; "doing" from an innocently contaminated mindset and the feelings of stress and urgency that often come with it. When you're "doing nothing", your actions are sponsored by clarity and understanding.

So does that mean you should only take action when you're seeing clearly? Definitely not.

Stay in the game

Woody Allen famously said that 80% of success is showing up. While it's great to feel intrinsically motivated, take inspired action and get into the zone, it's surprising how often the inspiration waits until you're already in the game before it shows up.

My dear friend and colleague, *Stillpower* author Garret Kramer, works with senior executives and professional athletes to help them improve performance and get the results they desire. Neither group has the luxury of sitting around waiting for inspiration to strike – they need to show up, ready to work when their team needs them. Whether they're seeing things clearly or lost in contaminated thinking, Garret's advice is the same; stay in the game!

When we're willing to show up, despite our insecurities, we create new possibilities.

While inspired action feels great, sometimes you just need to "do the right thing", in spite of your contaminated thinking. As you continue allowing yourself to become more responsive to your wisdom, you'll often find that the answers you need come at the exact moment you need them.

Sometimes the "right thing to do" is to take a specific action.

Sometimes the "right thing to do" is to stop and take a rest.

Sometimes the "right thing to do" is to wait for further guidance.

In the meantime, stay in the game!

But what about those times when you need to make a decision immediately, and you're not getting a clear steer from your wisdom one way or another? In those situations, you make the best decision you can based on the information available. These are exactly the moments when the best thing you've got going for you is clarity. When all other factors are equal, the person with the clearest head is holding the strongest hand.

The actions we take are informed by our understanding of how life works, and serve to reinforce that understanding. When we act from the outside-in misunderstanding, the actions we take reinforce that misunderstanding. When we act from an inside-out understanding of life, the actions we take endorse that understanding. Even if it's the same action!

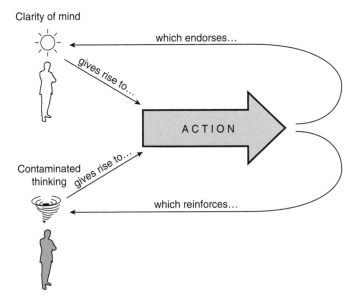

Figure 19.1 Actions Endorse/reinforce Understanding

So, when you're staying in the game, leaving your thinking to self-correct and increasing your clarity of understanding, a world of new possibilities starts opening up for you. Your increasing enjoyment in leading your own life may even inspire you to start guiding others in this direction. Either way, it's worth getting the inside track on…

---

keep exploring* ⁜ *connect with others
share your discoveries* ⁜ *deepen your understanding

Thought experiment: *How would your life be different moving forward if you were willing to show up and stay in the game, regardless of any contaminated thinking you may have?*

www.LittleBookOfClarity.com/chapter19

20

The Leadership Delusion

....

*"Leaders don't create followers,
they create more leaders."*

Ralph Nader, Attorney consumer advocate,
and political activist

"Here's the problem: Our business is growing steadily at 25%. We're taking on new staff every year, but we haven't found a way to develop new leaders at anything like the same rate..."

I was speaking with the practice manager for a consulting group that works with Global 1000 companies. His comments echo a sentiment I've heard repeatedly from company directors over the years, "We need more leaders; they're hard to find and even harder to make!"

A recent search for the term "leadership" on Amazon returned 93,606 books. All over the world, people attend programmes, read books and listen to audios, trying to master the skills and qualities of leadership.

But if the 93,606 books were looking in the right direction, don't you think we would have found the solution to "the leadership problem" by now?

I was working with a group recently, and we were exploring the subject of leadership. I invited the group to make a list of what they considered the causes of leadership to be. The list they came up with included:

- Vision
- Passion
- Goals
- Action
- Contribution
- Flexibility
- Listening
- Being decisive
- Stillness
- Teambuilding

While the items they'd identified are certainly valuable, they're actually symptoms or "effects" of the leadership bug, rather than the causes.

DISTINCTION: Symptoms vs. Causes

- **Symptoms:** Most leadership books and programmes make a valiant effort to help people master the "symptoms" of leadership; behaviours, skills and attitudes, modelled from successful leaders. Unfortunately, acting like you have the symptoms of leadership is similar to acting like you have a cold; difficult and unconvincing.

- **Causes:** The source of leadership is the cause that *gives rise* to the symptoms. As you start to catch the "leadership bug", you'll find the symptoms of authentic leadership start emerging effortlessly and authentically.

So what causes leadership? What's the "bug" that gives rise to these symptoms? And how does a person catch it?

- Good news: you've already got it; everyone has the "cause" of leadership within them.

- Bad news: for most people it's covered over, shrouded in layers of contaminated thinking.

- Great news: as you increase your clarity of understanding, you awaken your innate capacity for leadership.

Highway mirage

Sometimes, when you're driving on a hot day, you see a mirage on the road ahead; an optical illusion that looks like a pool of water.

The first time you see one, it's a little strange, but you quickly learn that there's no pool of water in the road. It's just a mirage – an illusion – so you don't need to take any evasive action.

Like the flat earth, the geo-centric universe, and the miasma theory of disease, contaminated thinking has *no grounding in reality*. Instead, it's grounded in the mistaken belief that we can feel something *other than* THOUGHT in the moment. But that belief is 100% false; it doesn't work that way.

And, like a mirage, contaminated thinking is just an illusion, so you don't need to take any evasive action when you notice it. Understanding its nature is enough.

The "deep drivers" described in Chapter 4 are the expressions of your innate capacity for leadership. As you begin to see past your contaminated thinking, the deep drivers shine through, and the "symptoms" of leadership start showing up. This is what's going on when people say that a person has "character".

If only I knew how...

One of the most common laments I hear from people is this:

"I'd follow my dreams and do what I want to do, but I don't know *how*."

This is contaminated thinking. Despite the sale of millions of copies of "How to..." books and programmes, very few people take action and put what they learn into practice. The "How to..." book has

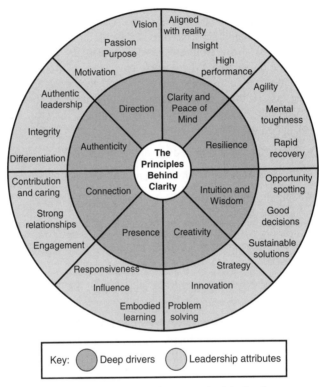

Figure 20.1   Innate Thinking drives Leadership Attributes

usually been written by someone who accomplished something of value, then shared the *symptoms* of their accomplishment (but not the *causes*). If the symptoms are like apples, the causes are the tree that grew them. When people buy "How to" books and pro-grammes, they're usually trying to glue someone else's apples onto their tree, without realizing it doesn't work that way! Think about it: To accomplish something of value and write a "How to…" book, you likely have to:

- Take responsibility for yourself and your results.

- Clarify your sense of direction, and find your authentic voice.

- Step into the spotlight, and risk criticism and/or failure.

- Look within yourself for security, resilience and persistence.

- Hone your intuition, and strengthen your decision-making-muscles.

- Develop your creative process, and discover the "how-tos" that fit for you.

These are some of the key elements of leadership. But the "How to" book can't give you these; *you have to grow your own*. When you look to someone else to tell you how to do what's right for you, you're accidentally giving your power away, implying that they know and you don't. Programmes that teach the "how tos" of lead-ership without an understanding of the underlying causes are subtly reinforcing the "follower" mindset.

Stop for a moment, and have a guess at how much of your working life has been spent lost in contaminated thinking. Now have a guess at how much of your colleagues' working lives have been spent lost in it. Now have a guess at the number of unnecessary conflicts, missed deadlines and botched jobs have come from all that contaminated thinking. Now have a guess at all the sick days and stress-induced illnesses that have resulted from it. Now multiply it by all the businesses in the country, in the world.

To an individual, to a business, to the entire economy; the cost of contaminated thinking is *astronomical*, not just in terms of lost productivity and unnecessary problems, but in terms of squandered energy, unused creativity and missed opportunities.

Fortunately, as you continue increasing your understanding of the principles behind clarity, you'll find your innate leadership capacities emerging and developing. This creates a strong platform for you to lead from, to create from and to learn from. You see, as you develop your leadership capacities, you can learn from any person, book or programme. You intuitively know what's right for you, taking what fits and leaving what doesn't. And this doesn't just apply to leadership...

Beating the bell curve

Every company (and every trainer) knows that there's a bell curve of response to any training programme. For a given course, some people will be deeply impacted, demonstrating genuine change, with new attitudes, skills and behaviours. Others will experience little or no impact, showing no evidence of any learning having taken place. The rest will be distributed across the curve, with most people being somewhere in the middle.

Your level of clarity is the unrecognized factor that determines where on the bell curve you show up...

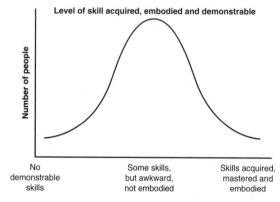

Figure 20.2 The Training Course Bell Curve

Traditional approaches to coaching, training and organizational change are grounded in application-based learning; teaching techniques, skills and methods, then encouraging people to apply them. While these approaches can be useful for routine mechanical processes, their effectiveness drops off sharply for complex cognitive and creative skill-sets. Why?

Because successful application depends on clarity, and the qualities it brings.

The CLARITY® model is grounded in *implication-based learning*, focusing on the foundational principles that drive high performance. There is no separate implementation step. As individuals see the implications of these foundational principles, implementation is automatic. Insightful understanding of the principles behind clarity *literally* removes contaminated thinking, and allows you to see more clearly.

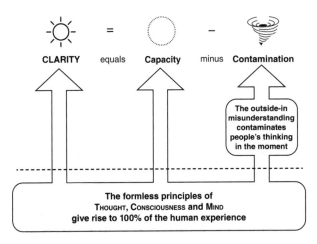

While there's certainly a place for skills training – I wouldn't want to be operated on by a surgeon who hadn't been to medical school – it's only part of the puzzle. I also wouldn't want to be operated on by a surgeon who had a head full of contaminated thinking about her marriage, her mortgage or her surgical skills!

So what is the leadership delusion? The misguided belief that a person can find the source of leadership *outside* themselves.

*The true source of leadership resides in clarity, giving you
what you need in the moment to deal with the
matter at hand.*

While there are certainly skills to be developed and mastered,
they needed to be grounded in the "inner" qualities of leadership.
And the fastest way to develop these is by increasing your clarity
of understanding. Because the symptoms are more "visible" than
the cause, it's natural that we get seduced by the idea of working
on the symptoms; looking in the direction of the attributes ("the
light's better here…"). But it makes far more sense to nurture
the cause.

You can nurture the cause by continuing to increase your understanding of the principles behind clarity.

And that means that something wonderful is possible for you…

---

keep exploring ⁙ connect with others
share your discoveries ⁙ deepen your understanding

Thought experiment: *What's it like for you to start recogniz-
ing that you have the source of the greatest leadership capacities
already right there within you?*

www.LittleBookOfClarity.com/chapter20

21

Living a Life You Love

....

"We must be willing to get rid of the life we've planned, so as to have the life that is waiting for us."

Joseph Campbell, Mythologist, writer and lecturer

"Now let me ask you something I think we all know the answer to: the test is rigged, isn't it? You programmed it to be unwinnable..."

In a pivotal scene from the 2009 film, *Star Trek*, a young James T Kirk (played by Chris Pine) is defending himself against the charge of cheating on the Kobayashi Maru test (a highly realistic battle simulation designed to gauge the trainee's response to a no-win scenario). Kirk is the first person ever to beat the test, but Spock (the test's designer) has accused him of breaking the rules.

Kirk's defence is that the test itself is a cheat; that if a game has been designed to be unwinnable, you don't have to play by the rules of the game.

So how is this relevant?

Here's how: the outside-in misunderstanding turns *life* into an unwinnable game. The "I'll be happy when..." and "I couldn't be happy if..." superstitions promise us that happiness, security and well-being are waiting for us "out there" in the distance or in the future. Whether it's five years, five miles or five seconds away, the outside-in misunderstanding tells us that our heart's desire is just out of reach, just out there at the end of our thinking. But it's not true and it never has been. That's not how it works.

When we look to the outside world for our happiness, security and peace of mind, we're looking in the wrong direction. It doesn't matter whether it's the "there" of material possessions or personal accomplishments, self-improvement or spirituality. The moment we think there's somewhere to get to, and that "there" is better than "here," we've stepped out of our sanity and into an unwinnable game.

So what does it mean to step out of the unwinnable game, and back into our sanity? What does it mean to live a life you love, regardless of its ups and downs?

The moment we stop looking outside ourselves for that which can only be found within, our whole world changes. As your worldview continues shifting from outside-in to inside-out, it's inevitable that you'll love yourself and your life more and more, whatever form it takes.

The search is over

Whether you call it the self-image, the ego or contaminated thinking, there's one thing it can't stand: the knowledge that the life you desire is already here; that you don't need anything else to be OK; that you can live a life you love, starting now.

As you continue deepening your understanding of the principles behind clarity, you'll see that searching and seeking is inconsistent with the knowledge that you already have everything you need within you; that searching and seeking is just another flavour of the unwinnable game. The very feeling we've been interpreting as "there's something I need to search for" is, in fact, the feeling of contaminated thinking, and nothing else. There's nothing missing. You were born whole, and you still are whole.

Reality Check

Am I saying that understanding these principles will transform the *circumstances* of a person's life into something wonderful? No. I'm saying that when a person sees life from a greater clarity of understanding, they have a deeper, more profound experience of life, *whatever* their circumstances.

Of course, when a person is living in a richer felt experience, and allowing themselves to be guided by wisdom, the circumstances of their lives often change too, but there's the paradox:

Once you realize your happiness, security and well-being isn't dependent on your circumstances, it gets easier to change your circumstances.

A practical example

Two people doing the same kind of work are both applying for the same position. Both are equally well-qualified for the new post. The only difference between the two is that one has an embodied understanding of the principles behind clarity and the other doesn't. When they go to the job interview, the contrast is huge. One is clear-headed, relaxed and alert, while the other is feeling anxious and insecure. One listens deeply to the interviewer, and starts feeling connected to them, while the other feels self-conscious and isolated. One is in touch with their wisdom and creativity, while the other has a congested, speedy mind. Who do you think is more likely to get the job? The person who feels peaceful, present and secure in themselves? Or the one who's feeling anxious, insecure and needy?

Life seems to respond in a similar way. When you are living from clarity, being guided by wisdom, life is free to unfold gracefully with each step you take. There will still be ups and downs; that's part of being human. But we've evolved to appreciate life. Our psychological immune system exists to guide us into a natural, enjoyable experience of life. Our natural response to life is gratitude and appreciation, when there's nothing else in the way. And what gets in the way? Contaminated thinking!

What follows is a list of gentle reminders to help you stay on track, living a life you love. They are not rules or "how tos," but they may serve to spark an insight or an a-ha that makes a difference for you at one time or another.

More importantly, they are not something you need to do, practice, or even remember. Everything you need is already right there within you; there's nothing you need to do to have a life you love.

Appreciation

When you find yourself in a more profound felt experience of life, appreciate it. This isn't a doing – it's more of a not-doing. Our deeper feelings of love, peace and well-being carry valuable information that can correct our thought-system, bringing it into closer connection with reality. So when you notice these feelings arising, allow yourself to stay with them.

Gratitude

Gratitude is like fertilizer for new insights. When you're feeling grateful for what you've already seen, you create fertile soil for new insights to blossom. Conversely, searching and seeking (with the sense of lack they imply) is like soaking the ground in weedkiller. Gratitude and appreciation are natural responses to insight, and to being alive, so you can enjoy them when they come.

Don't try to figure it out

Like the sun behind the clouds, your clarity, security and peace of mind are always within you, whether you're aware of it or not. But you can't *think* your way to clarity and well-being, so there's no point in trying to figure it out. That just creates more thinking, which is the only thing that's ever blocking your awareness of clarity in the first place. Instead, you can relax, and recognize that everything you're experiencing is a demonstration of the principles behind clarity in action.

Understanding is a rational goal

Everyone likes to feel good, but when we make that our goal, we use all our old habits of thinking to achieve it (with predictable results). When your goal is increasing your clarity of understanding, then every experience is an opportunity to learn; to see how the principles behind clarity are creating an experience of life in this moment.

Pause when agitated

When you're feeling anxious, insecure and agitated, your thinking looks absolutely real. But we're always feeling our thinking in the moment, and an agitated feeling means agitated thinking; nothing more, nothing less. While I don't recommend you do anything about it – let it change when it changes – your wisdom will remind you that you're in the feeling of the principle of THOUGHT taking form in the moment. That's the signal that the system is self-correcting. When that wise thought occurs to you, pay attention, and it will guide you back to clarity.

Look to the source

In any situation, we're either aligned with the outside-in misunderstanding (looking towards the *products* of MIND, THOUGHT and CONSCIOUSNESS), or with the inside-out reality (looking towards the *principles* of MIND, THOUGHT and CONSCIOUSNESS). When we're lost in contaminated thinking, it can seem like the only way of perceiving a situation. But, in any moment, you can look away from the results of your thinking, and towards its source, the principles of Mind, Consciousness and Thought. Once again, this isn't a do-ing, but rather something that happens when you step out of the unwinnable game, and keep waking up to your wisdom.

You don't need to be vigilant

So many people (myself included) have learned to be vigilant with their thinking, trying to monitor and manage their experience. This results in a bunch more thinking, which can block them from the experience of clarity, which is the very thing they were trying to get in the first place. You don't need to do this anymore. When you have an insight, it updates your thought-system. You don't need to work on it.

Be kind to yourself

If being hard on yourself was going to work, it would have worked by now. I encourage you to be kind, gentle and loving with yourself. We all have flaws, frailties and weaknesses;

you can love yourself as you are, warts and all. Paradoxically, when we love and accept ourselves as we are, things that used to be utterly resistant to change can suddenly shift effortlessly. Or not. Be kind to yourself, either way. Once again, this isn't really something to do; it's more something to be aware of and open to. As your contaminated thinking continues clearing out, you may start noticing just how much you already love yourself, but just hadn't fully realized it until now. (If that sentence makes you feel uncomfortable, do remember that you're feeling your thinking.)

Lighten up

Oscar Wilde famously said *"Life is too important to be taken seriously."* The *feeling* of seriousness is just a signal that we have serious thinking, but if we don't know that, it can be a grind. While there are situations that require a serious response, there's no need to *feel* serious about it. Love, peace and clarity often carry the information you need to solve the more challenging issues in life, and those deeper feelings are incompatible with the *feeling* of seriousness (though it's still fine to behave seriously when necessary).

Follow your wisdom

Your wisdom will guide you from wherever you are now to your most fulfilling, inspiring life. Wisdom doesn't make us immune to the ups and downs of life, but it helps us to live life in a way that fits perfectly with who we are. As you learn to navigate by wisdom, and deepen your understanding of the principles behind clarity, you'll find yourself living a life you love, more and more each day.

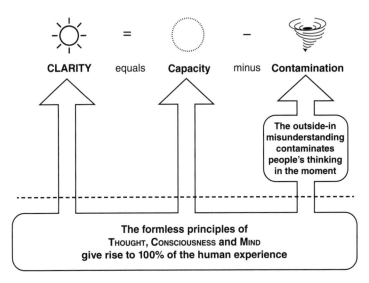

The power of principles revisited

Earlier in the book, I used the metaphor of a football being held underwater to symbolize a person's innate clarity, resilience and well-being. As soon as the hand holding the football releases it, the ball rises to the surface.

The reason the ball rises so reliably is because of buoyancy. There are precise factors that govern the rate at which an immersed object will rise, including weight, density and friction. But these factors are all governed by a single principle; the principle of gravity.

Buoyancy works the same way for everyone because gravity doesn't play favourites. It's nothing personal, and there are no exceptions...

In the same way, the principles that give rise to our innate clarity, security and wellbeing work the same way for everyone. It's nothing personal, and there are no exceptions...

So, if this is genuinely a "new paradigm", what does that mean for the world of business and work in the years to come? And what does it mean for us as individuals?

---

keep exploring ⁘ connect with others
share your discoveries ⁘ deepen your understanding

Thought experiment: *Have you already started to notice that any lingering sense you may have had that there's somewhere to get to (and that there is better than here) was an illusion? That the search is over?*

www.LittleBookOfClarity.com/chapter21

22

Capitalizing on Chaos, Complexity and Uncertainty

....

"We are at that very point in time when a 400-year-old age is dying and another is struggling to be born."

Dee Ward Hock, Founder and former CEO of Visa

"Everything that can be invented has been invented..."

A popular myth credits the 1899 commissioner of the US patent office with this quaintly absurd statement. Today, the world is changing ever faster. But what if there's a larger pattern behind the changes we're experiencing?

The waves of transformation

In their seminal book *The Third Wave*, Alvin and Heidi Toffler use the metaphor of *waves* to describe the revolutionary changes that have swept over the globe through history…

1st wave: The Agricultural Revolution (Domestication)
The 1st wave starts around 8000 BC with the domestication and farming of plants and animals, resulting in stabilization of food supplies. Over time, increasing agricultural wealth allows farming cultures with food economies to dominate hunter-gatherer cultures.

2nd wave: The Industrial Revolution (Mechanization)
The 2nd wave starts around 1760 with the mechanization of manual labour, resulting in the mass production of goods. Industrial wealth results in manufacturing economies that dominate agricultural societies.

3rd wave: The Information Revolution (Digitization)
The 3rd wave starts around 1940 with the digitization of information. The knowledge economy rewards informational wealth, and dominates information-poor industrial cultures.

The current wave-shift

There's a close correlation between adoption of emergent wave-drivers (domestication, mechanization, digitization) and commercial success. The individuals and companies that embraced the Industrial Revolution prospered. The early-adopters of information technology won a massive advantage over those who hesitated. In fact, the largest and most profitable enterprises are those that fully embrace the emergent wave-drivers (e.g., Apple, Microsoft, Google, Amazon, Facebook, etc.).

Early signs of the 4th wave

The "advance signals" of the 4th wave started arriving in the late 19th century with the birth of the field of psychology. In the last 50 years, we've seen the rise of the human potential movement, positive psychology and personal development. More recently, people have started identifying the need for emotional intelligence in the workplace, and there's an increasing desire for authenticity, integrity and transparency in the companies we do business with. We're also seeing the decline of many institutions that we previously relied on for a sense of security, purpose and belonging (e.g., religions, education system, civil service, large companies, jobs for life, etc.). As a result, more and more people are looking elsewhere for security, belonging and purpose as they pursue "portfolio careers" and move towards greater independence and personal freedom.

Understanding the nature of THOUGHT

The 1st, 2nd and 3rd waves have each been driven by an insightful understanding of the wave's key leverage point:

- 1st wave (Agricultural Revolution): understanding of *farming/ agriculture.*

- 2nd wave (Industrial Revolution): understanding of *mechanization/industry.*

- 3rd wave (Information Revolution): understanding of *information/digitization/computerization*.

The deeper our understanding of the "leverage point" within a given wave, the more power we have to create value.

- 4th wave (Thought revolution): understanding of the nature of *THOUGHT*.

The experience economy

There are already numerous signs that we're moving towards an "experience economy". As people become more time-poor, attention-starved and values-focused, the quality of their *experience* of life becomes more important. People are seeking out pockets of experience, like oases in a desert. Starbucks have built a multi-billion-dollar business based on encouraging people to carve 20–30 minutes out of an already busy day so they can sit on a sofa drinking a five-dollar coffee with their name written on the cup. A 20–30 minute *experience*, repeated daily for millions of people. The Apple Store has helped turn Apple into the most profitable company in the world by creating a brilliantly executed in-store *experience*, and introducing people to exquisitely designed, high-utility "lifestyle products". Adventure tourism (adrenalin sports experiences), sacred travel (spiritual hotspots for New Agers), extreme tourism (travel to very dangerous places) and eco-tourism (ecologically friendly travel) are all examples of people's willingness to pay for values-based *experiences*. So how does an individual or a business capitalize on the chaos, complexity and uncertainty that the current wave-shift is bringing?

The critical 4th-wave factor

There's one thing that affects the quality of *experience* a person has more than any other factor: your level of clarity – the state of mind you're in when you're having the experience. Clarity is "the difference that makes the difference" when it comes to any experience:

- A couple go to a movie. One of them is fully engaged and loves it (clarity), the other is bored and distracted (contaminated thinking).

- Six people are sitting in a business meeting. The difference between a grindingly dull waste of time and a productive, generative experience is the clarity of the participants.

- A family go on holiday to the Seychelles. Four of them love it, but the teenage son finds it tedious. Clarity is what makes the difference.

The value of an event is dependent on the quality of the experience the person has. The quality of the experience a person has is 100% dependent on their level of clarity when they're having the experience. This is why understanding the nature of THOUGHT is so fundamental to the experience economy.

So far, in the experience economy, businesses have taken responsibility for managing more and more of the external aspects of a person's experience. Video-game designers have taken it a step further, and are masters of influencing the neural events that their players experience. The future belongs to those who are willing to go one step further than that, and start influencing their employees' and clients' levels of clarity; their embodied understanding of how life works.

The reality of the inside-out nature of life has the power to touch our true identity; our essence; our spirits. And as we continue waking up to who we really are, we discover that the very thing that can make the biggest difference in our own lives also represents our most profound contribution to humanity, the world and to all of life…

---

keep exploring ⁘ connect with others
share your discoveries ⁘ deepen your understanding

Thought experiment: *The Industrial Revolution gave rise to a massive, sustained increase in the standard of living for huge numbers of people. This was a step-change unlike anything in humanity's history. Has it occurred to you that we could be on the verge of another, similarly profound step-change?*

www.LittleBookOfClarity.com/chapter22

23

The Art of
Sustainable Change

....

"Culture eats strategy for breakfast."

Peter Drucker, Management consultant and writer

**"We have developed speed but we have shut ourselves in.
Machinery that gives abundance has left us in want. Our
knowledge has made us cynical, our cleverness hard and
unkind. We think too much and feel too little. More than
machinery we need humanity. More than cleverness we
need kindness…"**

Charlie Chaplin's arrestingly beautiful final speech from *The
Great Dictator* (1940) seems more relevant today than ever, echo-
ing across the intervening years like a prophesy.

Artists like Chaplin are the canaries in humanity's coal mine, sensing our emerging patterns and potentials long before they become obvious to everyone else. And, while his warnings about our relationship to technology are uncannily prescient, his message of hope for our individual and collective future shines through even more strongly.

The end of the caterpillar's world

Once a caterpillar sheds its skin to reveal the chrysalis that will offer protection during the process of metamorphosis, the caterpillar starts to disintegrate, resulting in a kind of "caterpillar soup". This creative broth contains a small number of surviving body parts as well as a huge number of imaginal cells that have been contained within the body of the caterpillar since it was born. The imaginal cells start to join up, and the butterfly emerges from the caterpillar soup.

This metamorphosis from caterpillar to butterfly can be a compelling metaphor for personal and collective transformation...

- The blueprint of the butterfly already exists within the body of the caterpillar, "contained" in the imaginal cells. Similarly, the pattern of your transformation is already there within you, "contained" within the formless energy of who you really are.

- The caterpillar doesn't "work at" becoming a butterfly; it transforms in harmony with its pre-existing nature. Similarly, you don't have to struggle or "work at" transformation. Aligning to who you really are is in harmony with your pre-existing nature.

• The change from caterpillar to butterfly is a metamorphosis; a genuine transformation at the most fundamental level. Similarly, aligning to your most inspired and inspiring life is a genuine transformation; a profound reordering of your experience of life, and how you relate to it.

The implicit ability to understand the true nature of life is there within each one of us, like the imaginal cells in the body of the caterpillar. As we start waking up to that deeper nature, our experience of life is transformed, and we start to live in a new world.

Separate realities

Once we realize that our experience of life is created from the inside-out, it follows that we each live in a unique, THOUGHT-generated experiential reality. No two people live in the same experience of reality, and each person's reality looks real to them.

As you continue increasing your clarity of understanding, you become more and more likely to see the "psychological innocence" in yourself and others. Every person is doing their best from within their existing level of understanding. If we had their thinking, we'd be doing what they are. When our clarity of understanding rises, we act accordingly.

Most of humanity's problems at the individual, organizational and global level are the inevitable result of our current level of (mis) understanding. As we get a deeper understanding individually and collectively, we'll act accordingly. As more and more people start seeing through the outside-in misunderstanding, our world will change.

Thought Experiment

London's Wembley stadium holds a staggering 90,000 people. Imagine it, filled to capacity, with each person holding an unlit candle in their hand. Suddenly the lights go out, and the stadium is plunged into darkness. In the midst of the blackout, a single candle is lit. Everyone can see the tiny pinprick of light, and they watch as the light touches the candles of the people standing near it. Those candles flare into life. Now there are 10 candles burning, then 50, then 100! The amount of light from the candles increases, and now you can make out people's faces. Within minutes, 10,000 candles are burning, and light fills the stadium. Then 20,000, then 30,000, and so on...

The moment your candle starts burning, you increase the amount of light available for everyone, and the darkness is further diminished.

The world is changing more rapidly than ever before; old systems are crumbling as new ones emerge to take their place. And while there are more people on the planet than at any point in history, we live at a time when each individual has enormous power to take part in creating our world.

Disruptive businesses, from Apple to Zappos, demonstrate the truth of Management Guru Peter Drucker's assertion that "culture eats strategy for breakfast". Even the most brilliant strategy is reliant on people to implement it; people whose culture (the shared set of stories, values, beliefs, assumptions, understandings and worldviews they live from) means the difference between success and failure.

In her book, *Conscious Evolution*, futurist Barbara Marx Hubbard uses the term "cultural creatives" to describe people who are transforming and waking up to their true nature. Hubbard suggests that cultural creatives are the imaginal cells in the caterpillar of our civilization, coming together to form the butterfly of our collective future.

If this seems far-fetched, ask yourself this: What would your company be like if everyone who worked with you had an insightful understanding of the principles behind clarity? What would your world be like if everyone you knew had an insightful understanding of the inside-out nature of life? How would they behave if they already felt good in themselves and about themselves? How would they act if they were guided more by wisdom than contaminated thinking? I encourage you to create your own projections of what our world would look like from this new paradigm.

Just as the blueprint of your most inspiring, successful life already exists within your *consciousness, the blueprint of humanity's most inspiring, successful possibility exists within our* collective *consciousness…*

Your response to the desire for genuine transformation boils down to a simple decision. Do you choose to…

a   Play an unwinnable game, struggling within the outside-in misunderstanding, or…

b   Focus on increasing your clarity of understanding, aligning with your true nature and living your most inspiring, fulfilling and successful life.

It's worth taking some time to reflect on this choice. Contaminated thinking can be compelling, and we all get tricked by it from time to time, but it's just an illusion. When you decide to make it a priority to deepen your understanding of the principles behind clarity, you're aligning yourself more closely with reality, and with your true nature.

This is the essence of clarity.

We are all in this together, each playing our part in the unfolding of life, our personal and collective evolution. The fact that you're reading this book means that you're looking in the right direction; the principles that are creating our experience of life. Keep looking in this direction, and your clarity of understanding will continue to increase as you enjoy the powerful benefits of insight and realization.

Above all, remember this: we're all human; we all have our ups and downs. We're generating our experience of reality from the inside-out, using the power of THOUGHT. And while we don't get to choose the timescale, fresh new thinking can show up in any moment. And when new thinking arrives, our world changes.

keep exploring ❖ connect with others
share your discoveries ❖ deepen your understanding

Thought experiment: *What if there's a bigger picture here? Many forward-thinking business leaders believe that we're in the midst of a profound societal transformation. Could the fact that you're reading this book mean that you're an integral part of the "societal DNA" for what's to come?*

www.LittleBookOfClarity.com/chapter23

24

Inspired Action

....

"Forget safety. Live where you fear to live. Destroy your reputation. Be notorious."

Rumi, Poet

"Inspiration often shows up when you're already doing something else..."

So…
Show up…
Grow a pair…
Get in the game…
Stay in the game…
Step into the unknown…
And keep experimenting…
Pause and reflect from time to time…
Discover your "how" as you take the next step…
Remember, you're living in the feeling of THOUGHT
in the moment…
When your wisdom reminds you of this, relax…
The system is self-correcting…
If you find you're pointed in the wrong
direction, adjust as necessary…
Become willing to make mistakes and learn from them…
Keep increasing your clarity of understanding…
You're capable of far more than you think…
Because you are far more than you think…
Discover your path by walking it…
And be grateful for the highs…
Graceful in the lows…
And do your best…
To enjoy yourself…
Every step of the way…
Secure in your increasing understanding…
Of how the system works…

keep exploring ⁖ connect with others
share your discoveries ⁖ deepen your understanding

Thought experiment: *Enough reflection; it's time for some action. When you get to the extra resources area for this chapter, you'll find a version of the preceding page that you can print out and put up on your wall. There's lots of other good stuff there for you too, as your reward for making it all the way to the end of this book. Thanks for reading this book; I look forward to connecting with you in person or via the internet at some point in the future.*

www.LittleBookOfClarity.com/chapter24

Acknowledgments

....

I'd like to extend my heartfelt thanks and appreciation to...

All my clients, past and present, including the members of my original Inner Circle Programme, and all the Clarity coaches, consultants, trainers and practitioners who are with me on this adventure. Special thanks go to the inaugural Clarity mentoring team: Della Tysall, Don Deacy, Gillian Fox, Kimberley Hare and Maureen York...

Dicken Bettinger, Keith Blevens, PhD, Cathy Casey, Chip Chipman, Mark Howard, PhD and Garret Kramer for your friendship, wise counsel and sterling mentorship on the Clarity Trainer Training Programme...

The many thousands of people who have joined the Clarity community, and are sharing this incredible journey...

Tilly, Boo and all my family, my heart is filled with gratitude and love for you...

Jo Nicholls, you really are my greatest teacher...

John Wilkes, for who you are, and who you are becoming…

Terry Leahy, for your love, leadership and vision…

The wonderful team at Capstone for believing in the Clarity message…

Valda Monroe, for your wisdom, patience and utter clarity…

Rudi and Jenny Kennard, for your generosity of spirit and ThreePrinciplesMovies.com…

Robin Charbit and Ken Manning, PhD for your wisdom, experience and encouragement…

Michael Neill, for patiently pointing me in the direction of these principles…

Chantal Burns, for your love, laughter and unswerving loyalty…

Sháá Wasmund, for your love, friendship and hustle…

Christina Hall, PhD, for the magic of language and an open heart…

Nikki Owen, I love what we're creating…

All my teachers, coaches and mentors…

And finally, to Sydney Banks, for uncovering the principles behind the human experience and sharing them with the world…

Further Explorations

. . . .

These are the books I most frequently recommend to (and often purchase for) my clients and friends...

The Missing Link by Sydney Banks (Lone Pine Publishing, 1998)

Instant Motivation: The Surprising Truth Behind What Really Drives Top Performance by Chantal Burns (Pearson, 2014)

The Path of No Resistance: Why Overcoming Is Simpler Than You Think by Garret Kramer (Greenleaf Book Group, 2015)

Stillpower: Excellence with Ease in Sports and Life by Garret Kramer (Simon & Schuster, 2012)

Invisible Power: Insight Principles at Work by Ken Manning, Robin Charbit and Sandra Krot (Insight Principles, 2015)

The Inside-Out Revolution: The Only Thing You Need to Know to Change Your Life Forever by Michael Neill (Hay House, 2013)

CLARITY: Clear Mind, Better Performance, Bigger Results by Jamie Smart (Wiley, 2013)

You can get *The Clarity Activator* (a free audio-companion to this book) as well as more CLARITY educational materials, including audios, videos and distance learning programmes at...

www.JamieSmart.com

CLARITY®

....

Jamie Smart's primary focus is on training coaches, trainers, consultants and business leaders to bring the principles behind clarity into their work with clients, into their own businesses and into their lives. In addition, he works with a handful of 1:1 coaching clients and leads selected corporate programmes.

Clarity certification programmes

Are you passionate about making a difference? The *Clarity Certification Programmes* serve the growing community of coaches, trainers and consultants who are leveraging the principles behind clarityin their work with clients. Over the course of ten months, we work together on the three essential transformations you need to share this understanding at a professional level: 1) *Grounding* – deepening your embodied understanding of these principles, 2) *Impact* – increasing your ability to share this understanding with others and 3) *Livelihood* – discovering how you can make your living 'from the inside out'. These programmes are also popular with entrepreneurs, business owners and other leaders who want to bring an understanding of these principles into their businesses and their lives:

- *The Certified Clarity Coach Training Programme*
- *The Certified Clarity Trainer Training Programme*

For details, visit www.JamieSmart.com/professional

Clarity coaching, 1:1 intensives and retreats

Are you ready for real transformation; more connection, passion and purpose in your life? *Clarity Life Transformation Retreats, 1:1 Intensives* and *Coaching Programmes* are an opportunity for you to get un-stuck, on-track and start living with greater clarity in every aspect of your life, including your work, your relationships and your overall levels of happiness and wellbeing. They include...

- *The Clarity 1:1 Intensive*
- *Clarity 1:1 Coaching*
- *The Clarity Life Transformation Retreat*

For details, visit www.JamieSmart.com/personal

Clarity open programmes

Do you want to experience greater clarity in a specific aspect of your life? *Clarity Open Programmes* are your opportunity to have a live experience, deepening your understanding of the principles behind clarity as part of a group of like-minded explorers. They include...

- *Clarity for Business and Personal Success*

- *Effortless Influence*

- *Spellbinding Speaking*

- *Coaching with Clarity*

For details, visit www.JamieSmart.com/workshops

Attendance at most programmes can be live in-person, or virtually via live-streaming from wherever you're based. These programmes can also be run on an 'in-house' basis for larger organizations.

Corporate programmes

The business world is changing fast. Organizations and leaders need new solutions to the challenges of volatility, uncertainty, complexity and ambiguity. Jamie Smart and his team work with individuals, teams and businesses to help you get clarity, unlock potential and deliver concrete, bottom-line benefits. Jamie's corporate clients range from an SME ranked as one of *The Sunday Times 100 Best Small Companies to Work For* to a Fortune 500 business designated by Ethisphere as one of the *World's Most Ethical Companies.*

To find out if a CLARITY® programme could be a good fit for your organisation, either phone the office on +44 (0) 207 0998305 or visit www.JamieSmart.com/corporate

You can connect with Jamie Smart using the following methods	
Twitter:	@Jamie_Smart_
LinkedIn:	www.linkedin.com/in/JamieSmartClarity
Email:	clarity@JamieSmart.com
Website:	www.JamieSmart.com
Phone:	+44 (0) 333 444 1982
Address:	Jamie Smart Ltd Unit 4B 43 Berkeley Square Mayfair London W1J 5FY www.JamieSmart.com +44 (0) 207 0998305

Jamie Smart [J]

....

Jamie Smart is an internationally renowned coach, trainer, consultant and author of the bestselling book, *CLARITY: Clear Mind, Better Performance, Bigger Results*. He shows individuals and organizations the unexpected keys to clarity; the ultimate leverage point for creating profound and lasting transformation.

Jamie's primary focus is in training coaches, trainers, consultants and business leaders to bring the principles behind clarity into their work with clients, into their own businesses and into every aspect of their lives. In addition, he works with a handful of 1:1 coaching clients and leads selected corporate programmes.

Jamie's corporate clients range from an SME ranked as one of *The Sunday Times 100 Best Small Companies to Work For* to a Fortune 500 business designated by Ethisphere as one of the *World's Most Ethical Companies*. He has appeared on Sky TV and on the BBC, as well as in numerous publications including *The Times, The Daily Telegraph, The Huffington Post* and *Psychologies Magazine*.

Jamie lives in London. When he's not working, he loves spending time with his daughters, travelling, walking, drinking coffee and exploring.

For more details about Jamie's corporate and professional development programmes, as well as full contact details, see the *CLARITY*® section on page 197.

You can read Jamie's blog at www.JamieSmart.com and connect with him on twitter here: @Jamie_Smart_

www.JamieSmart.com